THE INDEPENDENT ACT
TWO PLAYS
BY MIGUEL MIHURA

THE INDEPENDENT ACT
TWO PLAYS
BY MIGUEL MIHURA

Sublime Decision!

The Enchanting Dorotea

Translated by
JOHN H. KOPPENHAVER & SUSAN NELSON

TRINITY UNIVERSITY PRESS • SAN ANTONIO, TEXAS

Trinity University Press gratefully acknowledges the assistance of the Program for Cultural Cooperation between Spain's Ministry of Culture and United States' Universities in making this publication possible.

Library of Congress Cataloging-in-Publication Data

Mihura, Miguel.
  The independent act.

  Translation of: !Sublime decisión! and La bella
Dorotea.
  Contents: Sublime Decision! − The enchanting
Dorotea.
  Bibliography: p. xxi.
  I. Mihura, Miguel. Bella Dorotea. 1987. II. Title.
PQ6623.I35A25   1987   862'.64   87-5020
ISBN 0-939980-16-9

Photographs by Peter A. French. Illustrations were posed especially for this publication.
Models are Lisa Isgitt and Francisco O. García-Treto.

Printed in the United States of America
Printed by Best Printing Company.
Trinity University Press • 715 Stadium Drive • San Antonio, TX 78284

Acknowledgments

We wish to thank Ms. Lois A. Boyd, director of Trinity University Press, for her patient and enthusiastic guidance in bringing this project to fruition. We are also indebted to professors Marion P. Holt and Gregory Rabassa for their insightful comments and suggestions concerning the manuscript.

J. K.
S. N.

CONTENTS

INTRODUCTION

Miguel Mihura Santos, one of the best-known dramatic humorists of contemporary Spain, born in Madrid in 1905, grew up in the world of the theater. His father, Miguel Mihura Alvarez, at different times worked as an actor, theater manager, and writer of musical comedies and one-act farces. Actors and authors often visited the Mihura home to discuss their work. From them, Mihura learned about the craft that he later made his own. He wrote, "At home I heard only talk about the theater, about applause, about song passages, about exits, about comic situations, about successes and failures."[1]

After completing his preparatory school education, Miguel studied music, art, and French; none of these subjects apparently interested him much, for in 1921 he gave up formal education and went to work in the box office of the Rey Alfonso theater, which his father had just begun to manage. Douglas R. McKay, in his study of Mihura's life and works, sees 1921 as a decisive year in the development of Mihura as a dramatist:

> At this juncture his interest shifted from actors to authors, a fact coinciding with his father's change in professional status. Paralleling this sensitive awareness of the joys or sorrows of stage artists, he now identified himself on a personal level with the writers who came to his father's theater to read or to rehearse their plays.[2]

Although he was not yet writing plays, the contacts he established with playwrights such as Pedro Muñoz Seca, Carlos Arniches, and Enrique García Alvarez played an important role in the type of humor he later would write. While these writers are generally considered the principal exponents of the Spanish theater of absurd humor, "their legacy to Mihura represents more an aesthetic conditioning than a functional inventory of technical resources."[3] What they all seem to have impressed on Mihura was the power of comic dialogue, from the absurd response to hyperbole, always seeking a new reaction to a familiar situation or cliché, thus making dialogue the most important aspect of dramatic humor.

His first play, *Tres sombreros de copa (Three Top Hats)* was written in 1932, but because it was considered too avant-garde, he could not get it produced until twenty years later. From 1932 until 1952, Mihura wrote newspaper articles and movie scripts and worked as a dubber for Spanish films. Some of his early movie scripts later would be adapted for the stage. During these twenty years, he did write three plays in collaboration with established playwrights: *¡Viva lo imposible! (Long Live the Impossible!)* with Joaquin Calvo-Sotelo in 1939, *Ni pobre ni rico, sino todo lo contrario*

(Neither Poor nor Rich, but the Exact Reverse) with Antonio de Lara in 1943, and *El caso de la mujer asesinadita (The Case of the Slightly Murdered Woman)* with Alvaro de Laiglesia in 1946. In 1937-38 he founded and co-edited a humor magazine, *La Ametralladora*, and from June 1941 to March 1944, he edited *La Codorniz*, journalistic endeavors that honed his distinct brand of humor and satire.

Finally, in 1952, two decades after it had been written, *Three Top Hats* was staged by an amateur group (Teatro Español Universitario). The one-night performance brought immediate recognition to Mihura as a playwright and opened the door to commercial theatrical ventures that he had been denied. In 1953, the play was awarded the National Drama Prize. It was translated into several languages—English, French, and Greek, among others—and established Mihura as one of Spain's outstanding comic playwrights. Until he retired in 1968, he wrote twenty-three plays, though none ever quite achieved the critical recognition of *Three Top Hats*. Part of its uniqueness, especially to the Spanish stage, involved the use of intellectual humor, disjointed dialogue, and absurd action, combined with the strong sense of human tenderness in its characterizations.

The play begins when an innocent, shy young man ironically named Dionisio arrives at a second-class provincial hotel to spend the last night of freedom prior to his wedding to a young woman from a conservative family. Quite unexpectedly—and perhaps for the only time in his life—Dionisio is confronted with the magical, fantasy world of a troupe of touring theater performers. During his encounter with these strange characters, who assume he is a juggler because of the three top hats he is trying on for the wedding ceremony, Dionisio meets and falls in love with Paula, one of the dancers traveling with the troupe. Although Paula is attracted by Dionisio's innocence and naîveté, in the end she declines his invitation to run away with him, and thus Dionisio returns to his conventional reality while Paula remains in her seemingly make-believe existence. In his comments about this play, Marion P. Holt calls *Three Top Hats* "...a sad absurdist farce." He correctly points out that "the special blend of the ridiculous and the pathetic, of gaiety and melancholy, and the subtle suggestions of the unresolvable contradictions in human experience make this play an extraordinary theatrical creation."[4] These very elements, however, perhaps explain the reluctance traditional Spanish "empresarios" initially displayed toward staging the play.

Though Mihura achieved critical recognition with the performance of *Three Top Hats*, his interest in becoming a commercial success seems to have influenced him to write more directly for the theatergoing public of his day. While reflecting a technical mastery of the craft and further developing some of the themes suggested in his first effort, most of the plays that followed lacked the experimental characteristics which made *Three Top Hats* such an innovative and influential work.

With the exception of *Mi adorado Juan* (My Beloved Juan), a serious comedy whose protagonist is generally considered to be the alter ego of Mihura, and *La bella Dorotea* (The Enchanting Dorotea), to be discussed later, the remaining plays published by Mihura have not received extensive critical consideration. These plays can be grouped in three general categories:

I. Plays of intrigue, mystery, or crime: *The Case of the Stupendous Lady, Any Woman Will Do, Carlota, Peaches and Syrup, Miracle at the López House, The Teapot*, and *A Real Lady*.

II. Plays about women: *Three in Dim Light, Sublime Decision!, Maribel and the Strange Family, Ladies of the Night, Ninette and a Gentleman from Murcia,* and *"Ninette," Paris Fashions*.

III. Light-hearted comedies and satires: *The Case of the Gentleman Dressed in Violet, Madame Renaud's Chalet*, and *Only Love and the Moon Bring Good Luck*.

These plays can be said to share strong beginnings, good development of plot line, and fairly simple resolutions intended to appeal to the noncritical public. They also exhibit another characteristic common to almost all of Mihura's works and particularly evident in the two plays included here: the portrayal of strong female characters.[5]

Perhaps the most salient feature of Mihura's theater is the combination of intellectual humor with human tenderness. This characteristic, exemplified already in *Three Top Hats* and evidenced primarily in the protagonists of his major plays, is present to some degree in all subsequent works. Even those characters who portray the negative aspects of a dramatic conflict, such as The Odious Gentleman, Aunt Rita, Don Claudio, have an understanding dimension which prevents a totally one-sided view of their actions or positions. This evidence of Mihura's belief in the basic goodness of human nature, along with obvious financial considerations, perhaps helps to explain his propensity for "happy endings" even when such endings diminish the strength and integrity of the struggle in which the characters have been involved.

Mihura's plots, generally developed along a single line, most often begin from an unexpected situation which the author finds comical. He then molds this in order to structure his themes and allow his characters to unfold. Even in his plays of mystery and intrigue, in which twists of plot would seem to be the prime consideration, character development often supersedes plot complexities.

The distinct brand of humor for which he is known, and for which he is often mentioned as a precursor to the theater of the absurd, is produced by a series of ruptures in the system of the expected: unexpected responses, dislocated expressions, absurd actions and situations, all of which the dramatist adeptly manipulates for masterful comic effect. His humor, however, is never cruel or self-serving, although it is used to satirize certain weaknesses of the human condition present at all levels of society. Rather, it is imbued with a sense of tenderness which aptly depicts both the frailty of our individual "humanness" and that of the institutions on which society places artificially high value. In describing his humor Mihura said, "Mine wants to be a tender, poetic, and sentimental humor."[6] He suggested: "Humor is a comprehending posture toward Humanity . . . It is not laughing at anyone, nor reproaching anyone, but rather having a caring smile of indulgence, of understanding and compassion toward everything."[7]

Beyond the works identified in this introduction, several other plays deserve brief mention because of their particular significance in his corpus. *Carlota* (1957) is an excellently structured mystery which has been favorably compared to Agatha Christie's work. While parodying the detective mystery genre it "presents a clever use of suspense, calculated enigma, deft manipulation of clues, and humoristic dialogue; but the play is more than a mere diversion. It is a work of considerable artistry . . . .And in its use of flashbacks and flashforwards it represents some of Mihura's most accomplished dramatic structuring."[8] *Maribel and the Strange Family* (1959), his greatest popular success of the 1950s, is frankly sentimental, describing the redemption through love of a young prostitute whose past is ignored by a naïve widower from the provinces. It ran for more than a thousand performances, was made into a motion picture, was translated into several languages, and won Mihura the National Prize for Drama.[9] *Ninette and a Gentleman from Murcia* (1964) became his most popular stage production, with more than two thousand performances. It also earned the author the Calderón de la Barca National Drama Prize.[10]

Sublime Decision!, written in 1955, seems remarkably contemporary in its depiction of stereotypical attitudes toward women and its satiric attack on bureaucracy. The play also introduces some of the themes Mihura later developed in *The Enchanting Dorotea*. Without being heavy-handed or didactic, *Sublime Decision!* illustrates the way in which human potential can be stunted or destroyed by cultural rigidity.

In this work, Mihura's skill as a playwright is evident in two categories: dramatic technique and satirical nuance. The areas in dramatic construction include the parallel (or repetitive) patterns employed throughout the play, the innovative conversations conducted by the women during the afternoon visits, and the effective juxtaposition of the home/office setting. The first of these, the parallel patterns, supply humor without becoming redundant. As in all good comedy, there are sequences that are not anticipated but seem correct after they have occurred. An example is the behavior of the office workers when Florita begins her employment. One after another, the men respond in the same way to Florita's presence in the office: at first they are uneasy—and this anxiety moves like a wave through the office. Next, they cannot find anything for her to do: another wave. Then they are charmed, and, finally, possessive. The responses are similar enough to amplify the initial effect, yet not so close that they become predictable or false. Mihura's expertise in these areas seems effortless; the scenes spin out as naturally as life, yet are delicately balanced and structured.

The two conversation scenes are not only parallel but have an additional component: they employ a series of choreographed duets. It is a technique highly artificial in method yet one which effectively conveys the social reality that Mihura has in mind. The women talk to one another across the room in designated pairs, with each conversation quite separate from the others. They chatter away simultaneously, arrive conveniently at a conclusion, switch partners, resume their gossip. The effect is persuasively accurate, a perfect rendition of social convention.

The physical structure of the acts is logical and seems inevitable, but when examined, it not only provides movement and interest but reinforces the thematic development in the play. The setting for act 1 and act 3, the middle-class home of Florita, is a "woman's world" of family and social visits. In act 2, the Ministry Office is the "male world" of business and enterprise. Mihura presents the two worlds as hopelessly entangled in convention and quite removed from meaningful activity. Florita moves from one domain to the other, relentlessly highlighting the falseness in both worlds by her insistence on some kind of integrity. Each act functions as a distinct entity, yet provides a developing contrast for the one it precedes or follows.

Mihura's satiric eye is merciless yet accepting. His selection of the precise detail that will best reveal each human flaw is unerring, but his acknowledgment that such flaws make up a generally shared condition prevents the supercilious distance of a satirist like Pope or Quevedo. The scene with the drugged cat resting sluggishly on Don José's knees is a marvelous comment on human posing. The absurdity and the complicity combine in some mad mixture that evokes instant recognition—we have all been there, have all worn the obligatory cat on our knees to impress the hoped-for lover (or employer).

Mihura's introductory note to future producers of the play is illustrative of an intriguing characteristic: the desire to extend the limits of his own inventiveness. His original plan to use the sound system as a partner in an innovative soliloquy technique had to be abandoned, but the description remains and the idea is engaging. Would a contemporary director use the simplified version or pursue the course Mihura originally suggested? On the other hand, the extended monologues by Florita, which provide more exposition than energy or effect, and the sudden appearance of one of the minor characters as a temporary narrator, pose obvious difficulties that seem ineffective rather than daring.

The conclusion of *Sublime Decision!*, a happy ending provided by a *deus ex machina* cabinet appointment, must be seen as less than satisfactory— as McKay notes, the final scenes "seem to have been dashed off with inordinate haste."[11] Successful comedy, like tragedy, should provide a consistent vision; Florita's initial strength and independence seem badly served by the convenient resolution of the plot. Nevertheless, *Sublime Decision!* illustrates Mihura's polished dramatic skill and his imaginative critical eye even when it also reflects his occasional refusal to completely come to grips with his imaginative vision.

The Enchanting Dorotea premiered at the Teatro de la Comedia in Madrid on October 25, 1963. The author himself directed the production, as he did ten of his other plays. From the moment this play first appeared on stage, critical reaction was extremely favorable. Alfredo Marqueríe, in a review for the theatrical section of *Pueblo*, wrote:

> Doña Quijota...Such is the title we would have given this new, tender, delightful, original, poetic and sarcastic play by Miguel Mihura. Doña Quijota because just as the Knight of the Sad Countenance sallied forth through the fields of La Mancha...disguised as a knight errant...the protagonist of this delightful theatrical work strolls through the streets of her native town dressed in a hardly customary manner...and is taken for a lunatic and for a rebel.[12]

Torrente Ballester, in his review for *Primer Acto*, finds

> *The Enchanting Dorotea*...in the best line of *Three Top Hats*, although naturally the procedures of 1963 are no longer those of 1936. They have changed considerably, principally in terms of the elements of verbal comedy, now much richer and accessible, and far removed from the surrealistic.[13]

The Enchanting Dorotea is an accomplished dramatic work concerning the inner struggle of a young woman surrounded by the narrowness and hypocrisy of a small provincial town. This juxtaposition—of the young rebel, Dorotea, and the society which surrounds her—occasions the creation of one of Mihura's best developed and most courageous protagonists. The gradual self-awareness she undergoes as a result of her impulsive, defiant act of rebellion against the established social conventions of her town is carefully interwoven into the development of the theme of the "theatricalization" of life that underscores the play. It is this very theatricalization — that is, the use of creativity and fantasy, artifice, and illusion, in final terms "art," to confront an unbearable, stagnant, and unyielding reality — which allows comparison of *The Enchanting Dorotea* with the theme of *Three Top Hats*, even though the treatment is quite different.

Dorotea pretends from the moment she first appears on stage. As the play opens, three young women (Dorotea's "friends"), motivated by jealousy, have come to harass her about her impending wedding. Functioning as the traditional "chorus," they represent all that is narrow and petty about the society in which they live and establish the conflict with which Dorotea must deal. Their absurd conversation concerning the weather sets the tone of oppressiveness dominating the atmosphere of the town. With careful staging, and the aid of Rosa (Sancha Panza), her maid and confidant, Dorotea transcends the situation by pretending that she has been asleep all night, thus denying the townspeople — represented by Benita, Inés, and Remedios — the satisfaction of knowing her inner turmoil. This initial scene, and the way Dorotea handles the conflict it represents, establishes a pattern which will be developed throughout the work: that is, the use of illusion, artifice, or theater to overcome the confining reality with which the protagonist is confronted.

Following the arrival of the letter which informs her that she has been left at the altar, Dorotea resolves not to remove her wedding gown until she has found a new fiancé to marry her. (See page 82 of text.) By daily parading her illusion through the town, she provokes the conflict that structures the action of the play almost to its conclusion. While Dorotea's response to being left at the altar can be seen as a passionate reaction to an unjust situation over which she had no control, her decision the following morning to put on her wedding dress/costume is a conscious act of rebellion against society; she determines to play out her role in order to conceal her inner suffering and to prick the conscience of the town. (See page 85 of text.)

After months of wearing her "uniform," as she herself calls it, Dorotea realizes that her "heroic gesture" has been in vain. Apparently ready to admit defeat, she is again rescued by "art" in the person of José Rivadavia, an unemployed baritone who arrives in Zolitizola intending to trick Dorotea into marrying him in order to gain access to her wealth.

Scene 2 takes place in a small park at the edge of the sea. A solitary sailboat off in the distance — while the cheerful music of the town's fair plays in the background — symbolizes Dorotea's isolation. Mihura cleverly stages this introspective, self-analytical scene so that the sea, the object of Dorotea's attention and focus, "we imagine to be in the orchestra of the theatre . . ."; the scene intensifies her separation from the town and directly involves the audience in her plight by extending the boundaries of the stage. This tearing down of the barrier—the fourth wall—between the "artistic" world of the stage and the "real" world of the audience is further suggested by Dorotea herself as she analyzes the role she is playing: "Actually, I'm no longer sure that's true. Perhaps everything I've told you is only the justification that I myself created. Who knows, I may be completely mad. And what you've just heard may be the tale of an idiot told by the protagonist. . . ."[14]

Act 2, like act 1, opens with the three young women—Benita, Inés, and Remedios—who have come to inform Dorotea's Aunt Rita that they have secured the necessary papers to have Dorotea committed because her "madness" is an affront to the town. The monotonous atmosphere is indicated by their repeated conversation about the effects of the weather. Dorotea now lives in a small hotel adjacent to the railway station. The occasional trains provide her only passing contact with the outside world and are the bridge between the closed world of Zolitizola and the openness of the world beyond. It is here that the artist Rivadavia confronts Dorotea. Costumed in top hat and tuxedo to play out his "farce"—in which he recites a ballad about a jilted lover which recounts the drama unfolding on stage— he presents himself as a madman who wanders the world in his wedding suit, bringing happiness to strangers by waving at passing trains as he searches for the bride who abandoned him at the church. Dorotea recognizes him as an impostor but she readily accepts the fantasy he has created as well as his marriage proposal in order to put an end to her suffering; through the theatrical escape it provides, she is finally able to remove her *costume*—symbol of her madness—in exchange for the opportunity to enjoy at least temporary happiness.

Although the final scene may be disappointing in terms of the resolution of Dorotea's conflict with the town, her wedding to Rivadavia does fulfill the thematic intent of the play by integrating and legitimizing the theatrical, or artistic, element into a new reality. Using the proceeds from the sale of her inherited properties, Dorotea and Rivadavia will build a restaurant, to be called The Enchanting Dorotea, in which he and other artists can perform.

The confrontation of the traditional, staid world of conformity (Dionisio) and the carefree, daring, fantasy world of the artist (Paula) of *Three Top Hats* occurs again in *The Enchanting Dorotea*. Whereas Paula chooses not to cross the boundaries which separate such opposing worlds, Dorotea, through strength of character and idealism, overcomes the narrow, hypocritical society which surrounds her by theatricalizing and finally integrating the artistic element into a new, open, and more complete reality.

The development of the protagonist, from a defiant, rebellious child into a complex, self-aware woman, and the thematic interplay of reality, illusion, and art through the metatheatrical devices mentioned, combine to make *The Enchanting Dorotea* one of Mihura's outstanding contributions to contemporary Spanish theater.

Issues addressed in the two works translated here are quite similar, the broadest of which is the theme of the relationship between the independent individual and a conformist society. Mihura begins with the recognition of two human needs: on the one hand, freedom and imagination—which he links to independence; on the other, societal support and order—which he links to convention. Conflict occurs, as McKay notes, when either aspect becomes "radical" or artificial.[15] In Mihura's earlier play, *Three Top Hats*, Dionisio is being smothered by social convention; he can barely breathe. It is a convention that stultifies rather than orders the society it should serve. When Dionisio encounters Paula, a person whose life suggests the complete absence of conformity and regimentation, he is forced to deal with his own life—and this confrontation illuminates the issues Mihura wishes to engage.

The relationship between the individual and society is also crucial in *Sublime Decision!* and *The Enchanting Dorotea*. Both Florita and Dorotea are independent characters who consciously reject the structures imposed by their society. Their background, however, creates a response different from that of the dancer, Paula. As women from middle- to upper-class families, they are much more tightly bound to social patterns; their vision is clearly influenced by their traditional lives. Florita and Dorotea are conscious of the loss exacted by their refusal to conform, aware of the power that conventional behavior commands. Still, they do not automatically acquiesce to the hypocrisy and injustice of the world around them. At moments of stress, both women strike out at mindless conformity and refuse to be shaped by a conventional world.

Emilio de Miguel Martínez, in *El teatro de Miguel Mihura*, places *Sublime Decision!* and *The Enchanting Dorotea* together as plays of "rebeldía," a sub-category in his general division of plays involving the conflict between the individual and society.[16] As rebels, Florita and Dorotea make trouble for the establishment. Both women attack marriage conventions, and in so doing illustrate the way in which change is initially conceived: not *en masse* but through individual insight. Dorotea, her pride ravaged by her fiancé's desertion, rebels by making literal what has formerly been figurative. Prior to her wedding day, she has paraded through the town in search of a groom; after she is abandoned at the church, she continues the search—but undisguised. Dorotea's anguish provides her the insight to judge a society that has previously exacted her conformity, and her pride enables her to strike out rather than submit. It is a desperate personal act, and Mihura takes care to create it as such rather than make it a conscious donning of a martyr's role.

Florita's rebellion contains the same personal elements. Driven by the winter day and the students' defection, Florita's pride also leads her to action. Like Dorotea, Florita makes a complex choice, articulated rationally but fueled by emotion. Both women, angered by the limitations that contain them, respond not with verbal protests but with physical acts: Dorotea will not take off her wedding dress and Florita will no longer go out on the balcony. In a society in which feminine submission is synonymous with virtue, such actions reveal what Mihura intends: that societal change may be discussed intellectually but is grounded in emotion and personal involvement.

Another characteristic shared by the two plays in this book, as well as *Three Top Hats*, is a satiric view expressed through a combination of standard and absurdist techniques. The most common target involves form that is no longer in touch with the reality it once represented. For example, social convention, originally designed to reinforce behavior that benefits the individual as well as society, is presented by Mihura as a set of rigid rules that has become an end in itself. Scenes involving Don Sacramento or The Odious Gentleman in *Three Top Hats*, Dorotea's friends or her aunt, and the visiting women in Florita's home are examples of this technique. In general, the language used is notable for the distance it suggests between the words being spoken and some reality those words might reflect. Martin Esslin, discussing the Theater of the Absurd, notes that it has "renounced arguing *about* the absurdity of the human condition; it merely *presents* it as being—that is, in terms of concrete stage image."[17] Mihura's absurdist characteristics involve dialogue and scene rather than philosophical pattern and direct themselves to situational truths rather than broad abstractions. His critical eye remains focused on the individual character and his or her relationship to an immediate situation; general extrapolation is possible, but has to be conducted by the viewer or reader.

In *Sublime Decision!* and *The Enchanting Dorotea*, Mihura's strength as a creator of realistic characters becomes his weakness when he declines to carry through with his initial insight. In *Sublime Decision!*, he gives us a strong and willful woman confronting a strong and willful society: the problem, though humorously handled, is serious. The resolution, however, is facile and unconvincing, and we are disappointed—in a sense, for Florita's sake, who seems to deserve better than a reprieve delivered by an altered government. *The Enchanting Dorotea*, though with better construction and with more persuasive—or at least more developed—detail, is similarly flawed. It is difficult to believe that the social giants taken on by these two rebels will permit them the endings that are delivered. Although the conflict in *Three Top Hats* involves the same elements, the conclusion lacks the easy resolution found in the later plays; Dionisio's inherent conformity ultimately leads him back to his familiar world, and Paula's world of illusion is seen to have its own limitations.

When Paula tosses the hats into the air at the end of *Three Top Hats*, we concede the "rightness" of the play: yes, we say, that's the way things are. Paula's triumph of spirit is human, limited, and acquired at a price. Dorotea's triumph seems miraculous; of course it is *possible*, but is it likely that José will arrive so fortuitously—or that any one other person can provide happiness? *Sublime Decision!* concludes with Florita happily rearranging the lives of other women, as well as her own—predicated on our acceptance of a fortuitous government coup. It is a conclusion that denies the nature of its beginnings.

When serious issues are engaged, the ending—ecstatic, depressing, or mixed—must be worked out in terms of the overall vision that initially conceived the venture. What will happen, the playwright asks, if a conventional man encounters a free spirit prior to his wedding night? If an intelligent woman cannot find a husband? If an arrogant heiress gets jilted on her wedding day? A facile plot may dictate a superficial ending, but once a plot gains depth, it cannot retreat to a surface level without creating a sense of betrayal. The women created by the characters of Florita and Dorotea raise serious questions about the way in which a hypocritical and corrupt society can destroy human dignity. They are strong, independent individuals who refuse to acquiesce to the roles that powerful forces would have them play. Once these characters have been brought into existence, along with the counterforces they will inevitably meet, the struggle needs to be continued at the appropriate level of engagement. *Sublime Decision!* and *The Enchanting Dorotea* seem weakened by the playwright's failure to address the pessimism inherent in the situations he has created. The world in which Dorotea and Florita exist mirrors a more cynical view than the plot manipulation evidences. Florita and Dorotea are rescued by external circumstances; the curtain closes, and we are permitted to leave the theater with a general sense of their well-being.

On the other hand, individual scenes in the later plays are rich in satiric subtlety and technique, especially in the use of minor characters. Hypocrisy, a constant target for Mihura, is attacked in *Three Top Hats* through The Odious Gentleman, who represents the use of distance between the speaker's awareness and that of the audience.

> Buby: And, naturally . . . being so rich . . . women must always love you . . .
> The Odious Man: Yes. They always love me . . . All the girls who have played at this music hall have always loved me . . . I am the richest man in the whole province . . . It is only natural that they should love me![18]

The satire is effective but the character is obvious; he is brought on awkwardly and does not function in the rest of the play.

By 1955, Mihura began combining the contrast exemplified by The Odious Gentleman with a gradual development of character that reinforces the effect and adds depth to the satire. In *Sublime Decision!*, the relatively minor character of Don Claudio is introduced in act 1 when Florita requests that he be summoned along with the priest. By the time Don Claudio actually appears in act 2, we perceive him as a possible savior— but are made uneasy by his introductory comments to the rest of the employees. By the end of the act, when Florita is fired in order to resolve a problem that is clearly not of her making, the satiric effect is intensified by our knowledge of Don Claudio's self-deception. His final speech begins, "I know, Florita, and I don't blame you but rather us, myself included." It ends, "The experiment just hasn't turned out well and I'm the first to lament it. Therefore, there's only one solution left. You must leave." The satire has moved from being a momentary flash of color to a necessary strand woven into the fabric of the play.

In *The Enchanting Dorotea*, the technique has become even more complex. The visiting women, supposedly Dorotea's best friends, are not only well-developed targets for Mihura's critical eye but also thematic representatives of the petty gossip that, like the constantly blowing wind, insidiously attacks the town—and the gossips themselves.

Sublime Decision! and *The Enchanting Dorotea* are engaging plays. They contain marvelously inventive scenes, absurdist dialogue, strong characterizations, effective structural elements: in short, everything for which their author is known. They reflect the maturing of a talent that secures Miguel Mihura a firm place in contemporary Spanish theater.

John H. Koppenhaver and Susan Nelson

NOTES

[1] Reprinted in *Miguel Mihura*, Colección Primer Acto (Madrid: Taurus Ediciones, 1965), p. 10.

[2] Douglas R. McKay, *Miguel Mihura* (Boston: Twayne, 1977), p. 17.

[3] McKay, 23.

[4] Marion P. Holt, *The Contemporary Spanish Theater (1949-1972)* (Boston: Twayne, 1975), p. 54.

[5] See Darlyn D. Davison, "The Role of the Women in Miguel Mihura's Plays," Ph.D. diss., Florida State University, 1974.

[6] Evaristo Acevedo, *Teoríe interpretación del humor español* (Madrid: Editora Nacional, 1966), p. 108.

[7] Acevedo, 107.

[8] Holt, 58.

[9] Holt, 59.

[10] Holt, 65.

[11] McKay, 106.

[12] *Mihura*, 136-37.

[13] *Mihura*, 139.

[14] *Mihura*, 228.

[15] McKay, 76.

[16] Emilio de Miguel Martínez, *El teatro de Miguel Mihura* (Salamanca: Universidad de Salamanca, 1979), p. 94.

[17] Martin Esslin, *The Theatre of the Absurd* (Garden City, N.Y.: Doubleday, 1961), p. 6.

[18] *Modern Spanish Theater*, ed. Michael Benedikt and George E. Wellwarth (New York: E. P. Dutton and Co., Inc., 1968), p. 165.

SELECT BIBLIOGRAPHY

IN ENGLISH

Davison, Darlyn D. "The Role of the Women in Miguel Mihura's Plays," Ph.D. diss., Florida State University, 1974.

Holt, Marion P. *The Contemporary Spanish Theater* (1949–1972). Boston: Twayne, 1975.

McKay, Douglas R. *Miguel Mihura*. Boston: Twayne, 1977.

Ward, Marilyn I. "Themes of Submission, Dominance, Independence, and Romantic Love: The Female Figure in the Post-'Avant-Garde' Plays of Miguel Mihura," Ph.D. diss., University of Colorado, 1974.

IN SPANISH

Cabello, George T. "El humor en el teatro de Miguel Mihura," Ph.D. diss., University of Arizona, 1974.

De Miguel Martínez, Emilio. *El Teatro de Miguel Mihura*. Salamanca: Ediciónes Universidad de Salamanca, 1979.

Guerrero Zamora, Juan. *Historia del teatro contemporáneo*. Vol. III. Barcelona: Juan Flors, 1962.

Monleón, José, ed. *Miguel Mihura*. Madrid: Taurus Ediciónes, 1965.

Ruiz Ramón, Francisco, *Historia del teatro español*. Vol. 2. Madrid: Alianza Editorial, 1971.

MIHURA'S PUBLISHED PLAYS

Sublime Decision!

Sublime Decision!

*The action takes place in Madrid,
in the year 1895.*

Note: In order to avoid the technical difficulties experienced during rehearsals, this work was presented on opening day and in all successive performances by modifying the stage directions of what we could call the prologue. When the curtain rises, instead of hearing the voice of the protagonist, Florita, over the loudspeaker, we see her onstage leaning against the flat on the right and doing her monologue directly, over the music in the background. The curtains, closed behind her, open at the moment indicated in the stage directions, and Valentina and Doña Rosa, instead of exiting by the door, do so to the right, thus avoiding the necessity of having a practical door and the passageway, which makes their exit clumsy. The scene on the balcony is also eliminated, since Florita gives all of her speech from the proscenium; when she is finished, she exits stage right as the curtains open and we see the set for the first act with the scene of the visitors.

The curtains work according to the stage directions and the musical effects are the same. For this reason the author recommends that this procedure be used when the work is presented. Many potentially hazardous technical difficulties that are possible when using magnetic tapes and loudspeakers are thus avoided; the effect is almost the same, and the exits are accomplished more quickly.

ACT ONE

A few minutes after the stage lights come up, and while the curtains are still closed, we hear through a loudspeaker—at full volume—the kind of dramatic music we are used to hearing at the beginning of radio serials. A little later, and while the music continues to play, the short curtain rises slowly to reveal the main curtain, which is still closed. The loud music continues but little by little becomes softer, sweeter, more melodious; over it we hear, through the same loudspeaker, the emotional voice of Florita.

VOICE OF FLORITA   Today, Monday, January 24, 1895, I have made a decision. A simple, everyday decision? No: better to say I have made a sublime decision. How have I had the courage to suggest such an enormous atrocity to my father? How can an honorable woman of my class have approached an old man like Don Claudio and so blatantly proposed to him what I've proposed? I still don't know, and I tremble with shame at remembering. Perhaps it was because it was cold and my street was empty and frozen and the north wind from the mountains roared past the corners...
[*At the phrase, "My street was empty and frozen," the curtains begin to open and we see, downstage, a drop curtain that represents the aging façade of a modest Madrid home. To the left, a practical door; and on*

the doorstep an abandoned child in a basket. There are two closed windows on the ground floor and three balconies above; only the center one is practical. The wind howls in the background as she speaks.]

At eleven in the morning, no one is in the streets. And as on all the bitter days of winter, a small child has been abandoned on my doorstep. But since all the other doorsteps also had abandoned children, people were not concerned and passed by him indifferently, chatting of other things.   [*From right to left cross Ramón and Hernández, two bundled up, older gentlemen who will be described in the second act.*]

RAMÓN   How are things going with you, Señor Hernández?

HERNÁNDEZ   Things aren't going too well with me...how are things going with you?

RAMÓN   I can't complain...right now it seems things are going pretty well.

HERNÁNDEZ   That's the way life is, Ramón...sometimes things go well and other times things don't go so well...

RAMÓN   Exactly, Señor Hernández...that's the way things are.   [*Exit left.*]

VOICE OF FLORITA   Heavens, what self-centeredness! And men always think like that. My neighbors from the floor above, Valentina and her mother, also passed by. The mother, who hates me, gossips about me—the eternal gossiping that all we single women do!   [*Valentina and Doña Rosa cross from left to right. Valentina is a young woman about twenty-five and Doña Rosa, her mother, is over sixty. She walks with difficulty, leaning on a cane.*]

VALENTINA   [*Looking toward the balcony.*]   Have you noticed, Mama? Isn't it strange that Florita isn't out on the balcony?

DOÑA ROSA   It's too cold to be out...

VALENTINA   That's true, it is cold...still...

DOÑA ROSA   Well, it really *is* cold, my dear.

VALENTINA   How dreadful! We'll have to listen to excuses! But it's not too cold to go out at night, when everyone else is asleep...

DOÑA ROSA   I don't understand what you're saying, Valentina. I can't imagine what you mean...

VALENTINA   Yes, yes...it's quite difficult to understand when you don't want to...

DOÑA ROSA   In any case...

VALENTINA   Of course...in any case...yes, yes...

DOÑA ROSA   Yes...what?

VALENTINA   Oh, nothing...just gossip...   [*Doña Rosa pushes the abandoned child out of her way with her cane; they both exit through the door.*]

VOICE OF FLORITA   Gossip! Always the eternal gossip! But what does she know about my life, about my thoughts? It was true, of course, that some nights I would secretly go out while everyone was sleeping...And it was also true that I would go out on the balcony every morning at 11:00, [*The doors of the center balcony open and Florita appears. She is a woman of about twenty-five or thirty, with an ingenuous and sentimental air. She is wearing a low-cut dress and leans against the balcony railing, while the voice from the loudspeaker continues.*] because in those days, a woman alone, shapely, with studied décolletage...leaning against the railing...would awaken turbulent passions in the neighbors, especially in the students at the Academy across the street. They would peer through the window panes, constantly in search of a delicious morsel. And the game was always the same...I would lean forward slowly with an indifferent expression...Later I would glance up out of the corner of my eye. [*She does everything she is describing.*] And the balconies of the Academy would explode open, followed by fiery looks, shoving, and some whistles of admiration from the bolder ones. [*We hear a whistle.*] And I, meanwhile, would lengthen my glances, smile slowly, arrange a lock of hair and twirl my little finger. But that morning it was incredibly cold and the students began an early retreat...and rather unattractively, in the midst of my flirting, I sneezed... [*She sneezes.*] But even so, though I was frozen, I persisted and cast a glance at those single young men, those possible husbands, and that glance became frozen in midair because the students had gone inside: the balconies were deserted...A tear of sadness rolled down my cheek, and I also abandoned the balcony never to appear there again... [*Florita exits. She closes the window. The curtains are drawn and the words of Florita continue without interruption.*] because that morning, Monday, January 24, 1895, was when I made the sublime decision that created the greatest scandal of all time. After begging my father to summon Don Claudio and a priest, I shut myself in my room, pretending a headache. I didn't even come out to see the visitors that we had every afternoon, the ones who chatted about such interesting and captivating things... [*The music, which has continued sweetly in the background, increases in volume and ends brilliantly. And when it ends, there is a chatter of conversation behind the curtains; then they open to reveal the set for the first act: the living-dining room of Florita's house. There is a door stage right that opens to Florita's bedroom. There are two other doors upstage: the one on the right leads to the hallway, to the kitchen, and to the stairs. The one on the left leads to the office of Don José, Florita's father. Stage left there is a practical balcony that opens onto the street and represents the one Florita was leaning from in the opening scene.*]

The furniture and the style of the room are those of a middle-class home of 1895: a piano, a bureau, a dining room table, chairs, rockers, etc., a seascape, many doilies and trinkets. It is 4:00 in the afternoon. Seated around a brazier in the classical arrangement for these visits are Valentina and Doña Rosa, whom we have already met. With them are Doña Matilde, Florita's aunt, a seventy-year-old woman, opinionated and autocratic; Cecilia, Florita's younger sister, who is about twenty; Doña Venancia and Doña Carlota—we don't care what these two women are like, so long as they are there. The conversation, which we have begun to hear before the curtains opened, takes place in a curious manner which leaves us totally unclear about what is being said because what happens is the following. . .which is also rather difficult to explain: Cecilia is seated next to her aunt, Doña Matilde; Valentina next to her mother, Doña Rosa; and Doña Venancia next to Doña Carlota. The conversation always crosses, forming a dialogue between the two persons who are farthest from each other. For example, as the curtains open, already speaking at the same time are Doña Matilde with Doña Venancia, Doña Carlota with Valentina, and Doña Rosa with Cecilia, which means that nothing can be understood because they're speaking very rapidly and in a screechy tone. But although nothing—or almost nothing—is understood, we will present the dialogue of the people who speak at the same time and who also, at the end, stop speaking at the same time, take a little rest, and begin shortly afterwards in a different order.]

FIRST PAIR:

DOÑA MATILDE   Well, I assure you I can't understand what's happened to that child.

DOÑA VENANCIA   Of course, Florita *has* been in a strange mood for some time.

DOÑA MATILDE   At first we thought it was just something she ate and we didn't worry about it.

DOÑA VENANCIA   But when she asked for the priest, we became worried.

DOÑA MATILDE   That's what shocked all of us. Don Claudio, after all, has known her since birth.

DOÑA VENANCIA   The thing is, for one reason or another, there's not really a single house where you can relax.

DOÑA MATILDE   You're so right.

SECOND PAIR:

DOÑA CARLOTA   So your relationship with Enrique is going strong?

VALENTINA   Naturally, and I'm so happy because, obviously, Enrique is very special.

DOÑA CARLOTA   Then I suppose the wedding will take place earlier than we thought.

VALENTINA   Our parents want us to get married at the beginning of summer so we can have our honeymoon in Badajoz.

DOÑA CARLOTA   And is it true they have many farms in Badajoz?

VALENTINA   They have three farms in Badajoz, but the most important one is in Caceres.

DOÑA CARLOTA   Well, you ought to be very pleased because I heard Caceres is a very agreeable place to live.

THIRD PAIR:

DOÑA ROSA   But when did all this happen?

CECILIA   Just this morning, right after she appeared on the balcony for a while.

DOÑA ROSA   I went by with Valentina around 12:00 and I didn't see her.

CECILIA   She was there a little before, and then she shut herself in the office with her father and said she wanted to speak with Don Claudio and a priest.

DOÑA ROSA   Maybe, as bad as the weather's been, she's caught a cold.

CECILIA   Who knows...she's so reserved about things.

DOÑA ROSA   She's reserved, but a good person; I've always considered her above reproach.   [*At the end of this dialogue, the three pairs stop at the same time; there is a brief silence which, because of its abruptness, is filled with general, isolated phrases by three of the speakers.*]

DOÑA MATILDE   Of course, of course!

DOÑA ROSA   Naturally!

VALENTINA   But certainly!   [*And after this brief pause, the six persons begin to speak again, now changing partners. Rosa speaks with Venancia, Valentina with Matilde, and Cecilia with Carlota.*]

FIRST PAIR:

VALENTINA   And is what I heard about the maid true?

DOÑA MATILDE   Yes, my dear, and you can't imagine the embarrassment she's caused us.

VALENTINA   It's even worse than I thought.

DOÑA MATILDE   I never imagined a girl who had been with us so long would be capable of such a thing.

VALENTINA   She never fooled me; I've always been suspicious of her conduct.

DOÑA MATILDE   But to do what she's done is outrageous!

SECOND PAIR:

DOÑA VENANCIA   Well, we're going to have to leave because it's getting a little late.

DOÑA ROSA   My daughter and I are also going to leave shortly.

DOÑA VENANCIA   We live rather faraway and by the time we get home and fix supper...

DOÑA ROSA   Well, if you're in a hurry, you mustn't delay because no mat-
ter how fast you go, it will take you at least five minutes to get there.
DOÑA VENANCIA   I don't know what happens but we're always late.
DOÑA ROSA   That's just what I said to my daughter . . .

THIRD PAIR:

DOÑA CARLOTA   Well, you really keep this room nice and warm with the
brazier.
CECILIA   Since this is where we spend all day, it's the warmest room.
DOÑA CARLOTA   The bad thing about these houses is the long hallways
they have.
CECILIA   In order to cross ours, Papa always has to put on his coat and
scarf. Because the hall is where you catch cold.
DOÑA CARLOTA   My husband, may he rest in peace, had the same thing
happen to him in our hallway.
CECILIA   All hallways are like that.   [*Again the conversation of the six
women is interrupted at the same time and, just as before, this pause is
filled by the three isolated phrases:*]
DOÑA MATILDE   But . . . certainly!
DOÑA ROSA   Of course, of course!
VALENTINA   Naturally!   [*And again the general conversation resumes,
changing partners in this order: Matilde with Rosa, Valentina with
Carlota, and Cecilia with Venancia. And as always, the six speak at the
same time, with the introduction of a slight novelty: all of them stand
up at the same time and, halfway through the dialogue, start walking
toward the hallway door and exit on the last words.*]

FIRST PAIR:

DOÑA CARLOTA   [*Rising.*]   Well, we really hate to leave so soon
because we were having such an interesting time.
VALENTINA   [*Rising also.*]   You'll have to come to our house someday
to see the new rug we've bought.
DOÑA CARLOTA   I've heard so much about it, and I'm going to see if we
can come by for a moment tomorrow.
VALENTINA   We have so many things to talk about because you know
how fond I am of you.
DOÑA CARLOTA   I feel the same way, and I'm always so happy to see
you.
VALENTINA   It's so nice whenever we have the chance to chat for a little
while.

SECOND PAIR:

DOÑA VENANCIA   [*Rising.*]   We can't delay any longer because it's getting so late.
CECILIA   [*Also rising.*]   Well, I hate to see you leave so soon since we're
having such a good time.

DOÑA VENANCIA   We'll call earlier tomorrow and you can tell us how things came out.

CECILIA   I think this matter with my sister will be just a passing thing and won't have any importance.

DOÑA VENANCIA   What you mustn't do is walk us to the door because you know how cold it is in the hallway.

CECILIA   Nonsense, Doña Venancia. It's our pleasure.

THIRD PAIR:

DOÑA ROSA   [*Rising.*]   Well, we're leaving too because, believe it or not, it's already 4:15.

DOÑA MATILDE   [*Rising also.*]   Maybe after dinner we'll come to your house for a game of lotto.

DOÑA ROSA   Please do—playing lotto is one of the things I most enjoy.

DOÑA MATILDE   I also enjoy it so much, but I never win *anything* other than heartaches.

DOÑA ROSA   You shouldn't worry about this business with Flora because it's all just nonsense.

DOÑA MATILDE   I think so too, but I just can't get it out of my mind.   [*When the six leave and the set is empty, the door to the office opens and Don José appears; he is a poor devil about seventy years old, prematurely aged and trembling from the cold. He's wearing a robe and slippers and goes to the stage right door and knocks while he says:*]

DON JOSÉ   Flora! Florita!

FLORA'S VOICE   I'm coming, Papa.   [*The door opens, and Florita appears, sad and melancholy.*]

FLORITA   Papa...

DON JOSÉ   [*Scandalized.*]   Did you hear what the visitors said?

FLORITA   [*Calmly.*]   Yes, Papa. Everything. I didn't miss a word.

DON JOSÉ   [*Furious.*]   I didn't either; and you must understand from what they said that your attitude is provoking quite a scandal.

FLORITA   I know, Papa...but we have no choice but to confront it.

DON JOSÉ   [*Even more furious.*]   All right, daughter. Let's not talk about it anymore.

FLORITA   Let's not talk about it anymore, Papa...   [*Florita locks herself in her room again and Don José locks himself in his office. The set is empty and the maid, Felisa, who is twenty years old, enters through the hall door. She carries a cat in one hand and a small package of pastries in the other. She knocks on the office door.*]

FELISA   Don José! Don José!   [*The door opens, and Don José appears again.*]

DON JOSÉ   What is it, Felisa?

FELISA   The cat.   [*She gives it to him.*]

DON JOSÉ   Have you given it the Linden tea?

FELISA   Yes, sir. Two cups, with orange water in it. And I've brought the
pastry. [*She gives him the package.*]

DON JOSÉ   Good, Felisa. Now go to the balcony and keep watch. When
you see him coming, call me.

FELISA   Yes, sir. Right away.   [*And Don José goes back in his office with
the pastry and the cat. Felisa now goes to Florita's door and
calls.*]   Señorita Flora!   [*Florita appears. She speaks emotionally
and happily.*]

FLORITA   Felisa! Did you tell Don Claudio?

FELISA   Yes. He said he'll come.

FLORITA   Was he surprised?

FELISA   Yes, very surprised.

FLORITA   And the priest?

FELISA   He's going to bring him.

FLORITA   Did you tell him to bring a good one?

FELISA   The best he can find.

FLORITA   Marvelous, thank goodness! I'm so happy, Felisa!

FELISA   [*Surprised.*]   Why are you so happy?

FLORITA   Don't you understand? Because I couldn't be more miserable.

FELISA   [*Without understanding.*]   Ah! Of course...   [*And Florita
shuts herself in her room. Felisa goes toward the balcony but is interrupted by Valentina, who enters through the upstage door and speaks to
her secretly and hurriedly without giving Felisa a chance to
respond.*]

VALENTINA   Felisa, I beg you...I can't stand it anymore...What's happening in this house? Why doesn't Señorita Flora come out of her
room? Why have you gone to get Don Claudio and a priest? Why are
you hiding the fact that Cecilia's suitor is coming this afternoon?
Why have you gone to buy pastries at the pastry shop? Why have
you brought up the doorkeeper's cat? Come on, Felisa, answer me.
Don't just stand there. Why does Señorita Flora go out at night...to
the downstairs apartment? Why have you hung that seascape on the
wall where only yesterday you had a religious picture? Why are you
buying a half kilo of fish now instead of your usual three-quarter
kilo? I'm the richest neighbor in this building and I'm going to get
married soon and I have a right to know...I can't sleep out of curiosity...I'm going crazy...   [*The door to the office opens and Don José
appears.*]

FELISA   The master!

VALENTINA   [*As she goes to the hallway door, smiling, trying to conceal
her agitation.*]   Ah! Good-bye, Don José. Good afternoon...

DON JOSÉ   Good-bye, child...

VALENTINA   [*With her peculiar sarcasm.*]   Yes, yes...child...

certainly!

DON JOSÉ   [*Puzzled.*]   Certainly?   [*Valentina exits through the hallway door and Felisa goes to the balcony. Don José goes to Florita's door and calls.*]   Florita! Florita!   [*Florita appears.*]

FLORITA   Papa.

DON JOSÉ   Did you hear the questions Valentina was asking?

FLORITA   Yes, Papa. Every one.

DON JOSÉ   So did I; and you see that the scandal is getting out of hand.

FLORITA   But there's no reason, Papa...All I've said is that I want to speak to Don Claudio and a priest...and speaking to a priest is not a sin...

DON JOSÉ   Why do you want to speak to a priest, damn it? What shameful crime have you committed? What's gnawing at your conscience?

FLORITA   When the priest arrives with Don Claudio, you'll see what I want them for.   [*She sits near the brazier and speaks in a rapturous voice. Don José sits at her side.*]   I can't wait for the moment to arrive! What I'm going to tell you is so beautiful! At first you won't understand anything, I know. Then you'll probably get mad and want to slap me...But in the end you'll see everything clearly and it will be easy and simple and peace will reign in the world and in the neighborhood...

DON JOSÉ   [*After a perplexed look.*]   Daughter of mine, I don't understand a word of what you're saying, but now *I* am going to tell you something that you will understand...I know full well that this chronic cold that I caught in that damned hallway is going to be the end of me at any moment...The few savings that we had we have been spending on medicine and herbs...At the office they only pay me half salary and soon I'll be let go...And as if that weren't enough, now you're doing this to me...Don't you understand that I'm going to die?

FLORITA   Don't be common, Papa...one doesn't say things like that.

DON JOSÉ   Why shouldn't I say it if it's true? The doctor told me I'll only get well if I have chicken soup...And where are we going to get a chicken? After that hat your sister bought, do we still have money to buy chicken?

FLORITA   Thanks to that hat, Cecilia has found a suitor who is going to come this afternoon to speak to you.

DON JOSÉ   But that still leaves you, my dear. And you're not doing anything to find a husband. We rented this apartment because the Academy is across the street, full of single students, and you won't go out on the balcony...Why won't you go out? Go on! To the balcony, to the balcony, damn it!

FLORITA   I've already been out this morning and it was so cold...

DON JOSÉ   What do the cold and snow matter if you can find a suitor who
will buy us a chicken? Out, out . . . to the balcony!

FLORITA   No, Papa . . . I've promised myself that come what may, I will
never again go out on the balcony . . .

DON JOSÉ   Has someone thrown water on you from above?

FLORITA   [*Sweetly and piously.*]   No . . . someone has thrown light on
me from above . . .

DON JOSÉ   Those idiots!   [*At that moment, through the hallway door,
Doña Matilde enters at full speed and with teeth chattering; without
saying a word, she sits next to the brazier to warm herself. She can't
speak she's so cold and gestures for them to move the brazier, which
Don José does.*]

FLORITA   Shall I warm you, Aunt?

DOÑA MATILDE   Please, Florita . . .   [*Florita gets up and rubs her back,
apparently a familiar ritual.*]

DON JOSÉ   Feeling better?

DOÑA MATILDE   Yes. I'm better now . . . Our farewell was too long in
that awful entryway. The wind was blowing and the visitors were
freezing, but we kept on talking until Doña Venancia caught a fever.

FLORITA   Poor thing, she'll die tomorrow . . .

DON JOSÉ   Just think of it, three people have died there already!

FLORITA   [*Returning to her seat, and saying to herself, absently.*]   How
long will these social conventions continue to take so many victims?
When will these visits be prohibited by the penal code?
[*Doña Matilde doesn't understand the tone and, somewhat frightened,
says to her brother in a low voice.*]

DOÑA MATILDE   Are you listening, José?

DON JOSÉ   [*Also in a low voice.*]   Yes, Matilde. It's malnutrition.
[*Doña Matilde is not reassured and decides to get straight to the
point.*]

DOÑA MATILDE   You ought to be ashamed! The time has come for me to
speak to you clearly, Florita.

FLORITA   [*Returning from her distant world.*]   I'm prepared for anything. Speak to me, Aunt.

DOÑA MATILDE   All right, dear, . . . I don't know what's going on in your
head but I suspect that it's caused by something you've eaten. I don't
want to place too much importance on it, because with the kind of
diet we have in this house, whatever it is will be cleaned out quite
soon. However, the reality is this: your father is getting old and
decrepit and could die at any minute, and you and I will be left in
misery.

FLORITA   Yes, Aunt, I know it all too well.   [*Looking at her father with
sorrow.*]   Poor Father!

DOÑA MATILDE   We don't have to worry about your sister because her suitor is coming any time now, and I swear to you on my honor that I'll trap this one...or if not, kill him, with the axe...

FLORITA   Yes, Aunt. He won't be the first.   [*Suddenly she laughs naturally, remembering something.*]   Remember that young man from Valladolid?

DOÑA MATILDE   [*Laughing also.*]   Of course I remember.

FLORITA   Poor thing! How funny!

DON JOSÉ   [*Bothered by this interruption.*]   Don't interrupt your aunt, child.

FLORITA   I'm sorry, Papa.

DON JOSÉ   [*To Matilde.*]   Go on with your lecture, Matilde.

DOÑA MATILDE   All right.   [*She becomes serious again.*]   But if you, in turn, don't find a fiancé and marry soon, the situation will be desperate. What with your sister's hat and the pastries we bought, we don't have a cent left. We can't take in guests. People of our class don't do that kind of thing—besides, we couldn't find anyone to take rooms in this North Pole—unless they were Eskimos. And in Madrid we don't have tourists like that—at least for now...You're not going to make a living by embroidering...or performing on the stage, either...

DON JOSÉ   That's right! That's right! Well said.

DOÑA MATILDE   There's only one solution: you must find a suitor and get married immediately.

DON JOSÉ   That's right! That's right! To the balcony, to the balcony.

FLORITA   But isn't there any way for a woman to live except by finding a man and marrying him?

DOÑA MATILDE   Until now, nothing else has been invented, my dear, and it's 1895, which ought to say something.

DON JOSÉ   You see? Get out on the balcony, damn it, before it gets dark!

FLORITA   But I can't find a fiancé, Aunt!

DOÑA MATILDE   Because you don't know how to trap them. You have to use all sorts of tricks to catch a man. It requires lying...pretending to be what you are not...deceiving, dissimulating. Winning battle after battle, with tenacity and without hesitation, like Napoleon Bonaparte...

DON JOSÉ   That's right! Learn from him!

FLORITA   But I'm no good at those things!

DOÑA MATILDE   Well, you're going to have to be, and tomorrow we'll begin the offensive. Tonight you'll fix the bow on your hat and tomorrow at nine, we'll begin the hunt on Recoletos Street.

FLORITA   [*Rises. And speaks again in a rapturous voice.*]   No, Aunt... tomorrow at nine I won't be able to be on Recoletos. I will never again be on Recoletos nor on the balcony...Tomorrow at nine, perhaps I will be free and the world will be different for me and I will go through the streets alone, without a new bow on my hat, without an aunt at my side, and without lowering my eyes in pretense of a shyness I don't feel. . . And now I'm going to my room.

DOÑA MATILDE   Are you crazy? You have to be here when your sister's suitor comes.

FLORITA   [*As she exits through the door to her room.*]   No, Aunt. . . I'm tired of all those intended suitors who intend nothing. . . I'm tired of everything and I'm going to my room to rest. . . When the priest arrives, let me know.   [*She exits. Matilde and Don José look at each other, stunned.*]

DOÑA MATILDE   As you can see, she's absolutely mad.

DON JOSÉ   Yes, Matilde. And you're very patient. . .

DOÑA MATILDE   [*She rises, resolute and purposeful.*]   Which means that we can't count on her for anything, and we'll have to devote our efforts to the other one.   [*And she begins to arrange the furniture in the room.*]

DON JOSÉ   Where is Cecilia?

DOÑA MATILDE   Getting dressed for the arrival of her suitor.

DON JOSÉ   Getting dressed? As what?

DOÑA MATILDE   The thing he liked best about her was her hat, and I've told her to put it on.

DON JOSÉ   But how can she be in the house with her hat on?

DOÑA MATILDE   She'll pretend to have just returned from a visit. Where are the pastries? And the cat?

DON JOSÉ   I have everything arranged in the office.

DOÑA MATILDE   Did the tea work?

DON JOSÉ   The cat is almost comatose.

DOÑA MATILDE   That's good. Otherwise, they get nervous and ruin everything.

DON JOSÉ   Do you think this cat business is really necessary?

DOÑA MATILDE   Indispensable. Without a cat and a piano, nothing works. Is Felisa on the balcony?

DON JOSÉ   Just as you said.

DOÑA MATILDE   We don't want that young man to surprise us.

DON JOSÉ   The poor girl must be terribly cold. . .

DOÑA MATILDE   Too bad! After stopping up the kitchen sink yesterday. . .

DON JOSÉ   In any case, go see if she's still alive.   [*Matilde opens the door to the balcony and speaks with Felisa, whom we do not see but whose weak, anguished voice we can hear.*]

DOÑA MATILDE   Felisa, are you there?

FELISA   [*Offstage.*]   What?

DOÑA MATILDE   Are you there?

FELISA   Yes, Señora...

DOÑA MATILDE   Can you see him yet?

FELISA   Not yet.

DOÑA MATILDE   Let us know.

FELISA   Yes, Señora.   [*Matilde closes the balcony door again and speaks to Don José.*]

DOÑA MATILDE   She's alive, José.

DON JOSÉ   That's good.   [*Cecilia enters through the hallway door with a new dress and a large hat.*]

CECILIA   I'm ready, Aunt. How do I look?

DOÑA MATILDE   Is that just the way you looked before?

CECILIA   Yes.

DOÑA MATILDE   Good. It's best not to change. If he liked you that way once, you must stay that way. The slightest alteration might disappoint him. And say the same things you said the afternoon he met you.

CECILIA   The same things?

DOÑA MATILDE   Exactly the same things, in exactly the same way. That's the secret. Don't try to be original and use new phrases. Men always like to sit in the same chair...

DON JOSÉ   That's right, that's right. Your aunt is right...   [*At that moment the balcony door opens and Felisa appears; her face is purple from the cold. When she opens her mouth to speak, her breath is visible.*]

FELISA   He's coming! But he's not alone. There are two of them. They're now at the door...way.   [*The word doorway is pronounced in two beats: the first syllable while standing, and the second on a chair where she has collapsed because the cold has consumed her. The family goes toward her.*]

CECILIA   Felisa!

DOÑA MATILDE   What's wrong?

DON JOSÉ   She's fainted from the cold.

DOÑA MATILDE   [*To Cecilia.*]   Hurry up! Get the cognac bottle!   [*Cecilia goes to the bureau and gets the cognac.*]

DOÑA MATILDE   Felisa! Wake up!

DON JOSÉ   [*Taking one of her hands.*]   She's frozen!

DOÑA MATILDE   [*Forcing her to drink from the cognac bottle Cecilia hands her.*]   Drink, Felisa.   [*She forces her to take a swallow.*]

CECILIA   She's not coming around...

DOÑA MATILDE   Take another swallow.   [*Again forces her to drink.*]

DON JOSÉ   It might go to her head...

DOÑA MATILDE   She has to get the door, no matter what. Otherwise they'll think we don't even have a maid.   [*Felisa is starting to give signs of life. She sits up, sighs.*]

DON JOSÉ   I think she's going to be all right . . . thank goodness.

DOÑA MATILDE   Come on, Felisa . . . don't just sit there. Get up . . . [*Cecilia kneels at her side and speaks to her in a slightly pleading tone.*]

CECILIA   Please, Felisa, you must do this. For me. Make an effort. I've always taken your part against everyone, and this is my big chance. If you go open the door, I'll give you a piece of that red ribbon you like so well.

FELISA   [*Smiles in anticipation.*]   Really?

CECILIA   Yes. Just think what this visit means to me and to the whole family . . .

FELISA   Yes, Señorita, I know it too well . . .

CECILIA   Let me help you . . .   [*Cecilia helps her get up. Felisa, once standing, staggers slightly.*]

DOÑA MATILDE   They must be at the door . . .

CECILIA   You have to open it, Felisa.

DOÑA MATILDE   Do you feel better?

FELISA   Yes . . . I think I can make it to the door . . . now I'm very warm.

DOÑA MATILDE   Don't waste time . . .

FELISA   I'm not, I'm going.

DOÑA MATILDE   Bring them in here . . .

FELISA   Yes, Señora.   [*With a great deal of difficulty she goes to the hallway door and exits.*]

DOÑA MATILDE   You, Cecilia, get the cat and the pastries from the office . . . unwrap the pastries and put them on the plate.

CECILIA   Yes, Aunt.   [*Cecilia exits through the office door and returns with what was requested while Matilde opens the piano and puts a piece of sheet music out.*]

DON JOSÉ   What I don't understand is why there are two of them . . .

DOÑA MATILDE   Just be quiet and sit down there . . .   [*She points to the chair where Don José normally sits.*]

CECILIA   What if the other one is his father who is coming to ask for my hand!   [*Matilde picks up the cat and puts it on Don José's knees while Cecilia arranges the pastry on a dish and hides the wrapping paper.*]

DOÑA MATILDE   We'll find out, child . . . leave the pastries on the bureau and you, José, sit quietly with the cat on your knees. Stroke his back and look pleasant . . .   [*José does what he is told and assumes a pleasant expression.*]

DOÑA MATILDE   That's right.   [*Once she has José prepared, Doña Matilde sits at the piano bench.*]   Hurry up, Cecilia. Put those pastries down and come here to turn the pages for me.   [*Doña Matilde*

*begins to play a nocturne by Chopin while Cecilia, standing by her side,
turns the pages for her and Don José, with a peaceful and happy expression like theirs, strokes the cat, completing a beautiful family picture.
Soon Felisa appears at the hallway door. The cognac has gone to her
head; she's silly and smiling.*]

FELISA   Señora... here are four gentlemen asking for the Señorita...

DON JOSÉ   [*Very surprised.*]   Four?

DOÑA MATILDE   [*Also surprised.*]   Didn't you say two?

FELISA   But now there are four... how funny!   [*She gives a burst of
laughter and sits happily in a chair.*]

CECILIA   But Felisa!

DOÑA MATILDE   Idiot!

DON JOSÉ   She's drunk!...

DOÑA MATILDE   [*To Cecilia.*]   Take her to the kitchen and then go get
them. How shameful! I'll have to come up with some excuse!

CECILIA   [*Takes Felisa by the arm and lifts her.*]   Come with me,
Felisa...

FELISA   Where?

CECILIA   To the kitchen!

FELISA   [*Very happy.*]   Oh, yes. Of course I want to go to the
kitchen...   [*They both exit through the hallway door. Matilde, smiling happily, continues playing the piano while she says in a sinister
voice:*]

DOÑA MATILDE   Yesterday she plugged up the sink and now this... I'll
have to bring her before the Council of War.

DON JOSÉ   For heaven's sake, Matilde!

DOÑA MATILDE   The Supreme Ministry of Justice.   [*Through the hallway door Cecilia appears, followed by Pablo Meléndez and Manolo
Estévez. They are two modestly dressed young men in their twenties;
they also show the effects of the cold in the hallway.*]

CECILIA   Please come this way... I'm going to introduce you to my
father and my auntie...   [*To Manolo.*]   What did you say your
friend's name was?

MANOLO   Pablo Meléndez.

CECILIA   [*Introducing them.*]   Pablo Meléndez... and this is Manolo
Estévez, whom I've told you about.

DON JOSÉ   It's an honor to have you in my home...

MANOLO   Pleased to meet you.   [*During the introductions, Matilde has
continued playing the piano, though she has nodded and smiled the
whole time. And now she says:*]

DOÑA MATILDE   Please sit down, gentlemen, while I finish playing this
beautiful nocturne... come over here, Cecilia; continue turning the
pages...   [*The young men sit down. Cecilia takes her place next to*

her aunt who, while she plays, says:]   Cecilia has just returned from
a visit to the home of the Duke of Montpellier. That's why she's
wearing a hat.

MANOLO   No matter, it's such a pretty hat...

DOÑA MATILDE   Beautiful...   [*She continues playing.*]   Oh, in this
house, we're such music lovers!...Music elevates the soul!...   [*To
Cecilia.*]   How well you turn pages, child! You're marvelous.

CECILIA   [*Blushing.*]   Please, Aunt...

DOÑA MATILDE   [*After finishing the piece, she pauses a few seconds,
moved.*]   How exquisite!   [*With effort, she recovers from her musical ecstasy and, after receiving the applause of Don José, she closes the
piano and takes a seat next to the young men.*]   Well, my friends...
[*To Manolo.*]   Cecilia has praised you so much to me, Señor
Estévez...but I see she hasn't done you justice. Isn't that right,
José?

DON JOSÉ   I've never seen such a charming gentleman...

DOÑA MATILDE   And such presence...

MANOLO   Thank you, Señora. I met Cecilia at the home of the Señoritas
Revuelta...

DOÑA MATILDE   Oh, yes! I find them a little flighty...don't you agree,
José?

DON JOSÉ   Yes; and I've also heard they're rather messy.

DOÑA MATILDE   We, on the other hand, are just the opposite...Lovers
of order, home, and music...Have you noticed our cat?

MANOLO   No.

DOÑA MATILDE   That's it.

DON JOSÉ   It's this thing on my knees.

MANOLO   Oh, yes! It's very beautiful...

DOÑA MATILDE   [*Serious and sententious.*]   Listen, young man, to what
I'm going to say: a cat asleep on the lap of a woman or on the knees
of a man symbolizes the peace and the happiness of a home which
every unmarried man should aspire to...   [*At that moment, Felisa
appears through the hallway door. The alcohol has gone to her head;
she now lives in a smiling world previously unknown to her. She greets
the visitors.*]

FELISA   Good afternoon...

MANOLO   [*Surprised.*]   Good afternoon...   [*Felisa goes to the bureau
where the bottle of cognac was placed and takes a long swig. She then
says good-bye and exits through the office door.*]

FELISA   Good-bye...

MANOLO   Good-bye...   [*Manolo and Pablo don't know how to react, but
Matilde saves the shocking situation with a smile.*]

DOÑA MATILDE   You're probably surprised by the behavior of that maid, but don't assume she's had too much to drink. Not at all. The truth is, she has meningitis. . .isn't that right, José?

DON JOSÉ   Yes, that's right.

DOÑA MATILDE   Cecilia, who is such a good person, found her one day in the street, abandoned in a doorway. . .with her meningitis. . .and since my niece is so soft-hearted, she brought her here to take care of her. . .

DON JOSÉ   Every time Cecilia goes out on the street, she brings back two or three people with meningitis. . .

MANOLO   And Cecilia, besides having a heart of gold, has a very pretty hat.

DOÑA MATILDE   That's quite true.

MANOLO   [Moved.]   From the first moment I saw her in that hat, I don't know what came over me. . .

CECILIA   You're very gallant, Manolo.

MANOLO   It's only the truth.   [There's a short pause, during which all of them smile at each other without knowing what to say until Cecilia suddenly says:]

CECILIA   Well, I've heard Santa Cruz de Tenerife is very pretty.

DON JOSÉ   [As surprised as the rest.]   What are you saying, child?

DOÑA MATILDE   Did you say something, dear?

CECILIA   Yes. I was saying that I've heard that Santa Cruz de Tenerife is very pretty. . .

MANOLO   [Finally remembering, and almost jumping with joy.]   Oh, yes!   [To Cecilia.]   Now I remember. You said that the afternoon that we met. . .And those words were so pleasing to me, since my mother is from there. . .

DOÑA MATILDE   Cecilia always says such pleasing. . .

DON JOSÉ   One mustn't forget that we've given her the best education because, fortunately, our means permit. . .

DOÑA MATILDE   Naturally. . .   [There's another pause in the conversation that Cecilia again breaks.]

CECILIA   I used to really like dolls, but now I don't like them as much. [When all of them are again surprised, Manolo says joyously:]

MANOLO   That's right! You also said so that afternoon. . .and it pleased me very much. . .

DOÑA MATILDE   She's so ingenious. . .well, dear. . .and why don't you offer these nice gentlemen some pastries?

CECILIA   [Going to the bureau.]   Of course. I'm so forgetful. . .

DOÑA MATILDE   [To Pablo, who looks at her without uttering a word.] And you? Do you speak our language, or perhaps. . .?

PABLO   Yes, of course.

DOÑA MATILDE   Ah! When you didn't say anything, I thought. . .

MANOLO   He's a little shy...

PABLO   Also, it's so cold, I was afraid to open my mouth.

DON JOSÉ   Cold? But I'm sweating something awful!

PABLO   Yes, but that's because of the cat, perhaps.

DON JOSÉ   No...on the contrary, the cat is turning cold.

DOÑA MATILDE   Go ahead, take a pastry and you'll start to warm up... [*Pablo and Manolo avidly eat the pastries Cecilia has placed on the table.*]

MANOLO   They're very good...

DOÑA MATILDE   Aren't they, though...Cecilia made them!

PABLO   Is that right?

MANOLO   That's impossible!

DOÑA MATILDE   Not at all...no one is better at making pastries than Cecilia.

DON JOSÉ   And if you only knew how well she cooks! Today she's fixed us a rabbit!

DOÑA MATILDE   José, give these gentlemen a glass of the liqueur the child makes...

DON JOSÉ   The anisette?

DOÑA MATILDE   Yes.

CECILIA   Don't get up, Papa. I'll get it...   [*She goes to pick up the bottle and glasses from the bureau and serves them while her aunt speaks.*]

DOÑA MATILDE   She's so accomplished in everything...She also made the bureau...

MANOLO   It's very well made.

DON JOSÉ   With drawers that open and everything.

DOÑA MATILDE   What do you think of the liqueur?

MANOLO   Delicious!

PABLO   Nice and sweet...   [*Once the young men have finished drinking, Matilde feels that it's time to get to the matter at hand.*]

DOÑA MATILDE   Now that we're having such a nice chat...just what is your purpose in coming here, Señor Estévez?

MANOLO   [*Hesitantly.*]   Well, I...I wanted to meet you in case at some time my relationship with Cecilia...became more formal...

DOÑA MATILDE   At some time? Why not today! You seem like such a fine person...doesn't he, José?

DON JOSÉ   I'm becoming very fond of you.

DOÑA MATILDE   Go ahead, make yourself at home...would you like to take off your shoes and put on my brother's slippers?

MANOLO   For heaven's sake, Señora...some other day...what I would like is another drink...

CECILIA   [*Pouring.*]   Why, of course.

DOÑA MATILDE   [*To Pablo.*]   And you, sir, if I'm not being indiscreet...

PABLO [*Also hesitantly.*] I'm a good friend of Manolo's...he told me Cecilia has a sister...and I've come because, if she's free, perhaps she'll suit me and I'll take her...

DOÑA MATILDE [*Shocked and offended.*] What do you mean you'll take her?

DON JOSÉ [*Also shocked.*] Your manner of speaking, my dear sir...

MANOLO [*Apologizing.*] Pablo would also like to get married.

DOÑA MATILDE Oh, in that case you express yourself very well, isn't that right, José?

DON JOSÉ Beautifully...

DOÑA MATILDE Well, yes, actually...Cecilia does have a sister, but today she's a little indisposed...I'm sure she'll suit you because she's very good and very capable. [*Pointing to a chair.*] She made that chair...

DON JOSÉ With its four legs and everything...

PABLO Well, if I could see her, in case she suits me...

DOÑA MATILDE Obviously, she'll suit you, of course she'll suit you...go tell her, Cecilia...she'll listen to you.

CECILIA I'll try...but she's so strange today...excuse me... [*She exits through the door to Florita's room. Manolo watches her leave in ecstasy.*]

MANOLO My, what a beautiful hat! And doesn't she speak well of Santa Cruz de Tenerife!

DOÑA MATILDE That's true...I've never heard her say anything bad about that marvelous city...

DON JOSÉ [*To Pablo.*] What is your financial situation, sir? Where do you work?

PABLO I come from a wealthy family, and I don't need to work. That's why, if I like something, I just take it and that's that...

DOÑA MATILDE Of course, of course...that's the way it should be. [*Through the left door, Cecilia appears, followed by Florita. The young men stand up.*]

CECILIA Look, Florita...here are the two gentlemen I told you about...Manolo Estévez and Pablo Meléndez, who also wants to get married.

FLORITA Isn't that nice. How formal! [*Pablo and Manolo bow.*]

PABLO Señorita.

FLORITA Please sit down...

CECILIA Yes, sit down, sit down... [*When Florita has taken a seat next to her father's chair, the young men return to their places and look at Florita as if she were a piece of furniture they were trying to buy. Florita twirls her little finger, but being stared at in this manner ends*] *up making her nervous and she finally says:*]

FLORITA   All right, so... have you looked at me enough? Shall I remain in profile, or do you want a frontal view?

PABLO   [*Confused.*]   Señorita!

FLORITA   Señorita, nothing! Do I suit you or not? Will you take me or not?

DOÑA MATILDE   [*Indignant.*]   Florita!

PABLO   Did you hear what I said earlier?

FLORITA   Yes, Señor. I always listen behind the door because I like to hear the nonsense customers speak...   [*Don José, Matilde and Cecilia become very violent at Florita's words, as do the two young men.*]

DON JOSÉ   Florita!

DOÑA MATILDE   Child!

FLORITA   I don't know if I'll suit you or not, but obviously you won't suit me because you have the face of a coat hanger...

CECILIA   But Florita!

PABLO   [*Rising, as does Manolo.*]   I didn't mean to offend you in any way...

FLORITA   There's no need for apologies. Will you take me or not? You must understand that I can't waste time because a gentleman from Barcelona might arrive and if he decides before you do...

PABLO   Señorita!

DOÑA MATILDE   Go to your room, child!

FLORITA   Then why did you call me?

CECILIA   You're completely crazy!   [*Pablo tries to apologize in a sincere and pained tone.*]

PABLO   I'm the crazy one because I expressed myself in words I shouldn't have used. But it's not my fault, Señorita, because my father is a vegetable appraiser at the market who buys and sells whatever he wants. I've learned to speak from him and I'm not ashamed of it, because thanks to his manner of speaking, he's a millionaire today and I'm his only heir... I suppose that some other day I will have the opportunity to speak more slowly, and I hope that what happened today doesn't recur. And now, Manolo, I think we should leave.

CECILIA   So you're not going to take her?

DON JOSÉ   Will you be quiet, child.   [*Pablo and Manolo bow.*]

PABLO   Señora! Señor!

DON JOSÉ   [*Bowing also.*]   Gentlemen!

DOÑA MATILDE   You see them out, Cecilia...

CECILIA   Yes, Aunt...   [*Cecilia exits through the upstage door with Manolo and Pablo. Matilde, as soon as they leave, cannot contain her indignation and goes to Florita.*]

DOÑA MATILDE   You've ruined everything!

DON JOSÉ   He was a good catch!

DOÑA MATILDE   A millionaire!

FLORITA   An animal!

DOÑA MATILDE   What must your sister's fiancé have thought!

FLORITA   He's not a fiancé...he doesn't even like her, only her hat.

DON JOSÉ   And what do we care...

FLORITA   They've treated us like two cauliflowers...how does this dif-
fer from the slave market? How long will women have to endure this
lack of dignity?

DOÑA MATILDE   You're going to disgrace us all!

DON JOSÉ   It would be best to leave you alone and never speak to you
again.

DOÑA MATILDE   Yes, that would be best. How shameful!   [*They both
exit through the hallway door. The stage lights go down. Sweet music
plays in the background. Florita pouts and then says, as if continuing
the story she began at the beginning of the act:*]

FLORITA   And I was left alone. And tears of sadness rolled down my
cheeks as I wondered if there would ever be a time when, in order
for them and their families to live, single young women would not
have to go out on the balcony and catch pneumonia nor stroll down
Recoletos until our feet were ragged nor have to lie to our suitors
telling them we knew how to make anisette. But I quickly wiped
away those tears when in the hallway I heard Don Claudio's cough
and the voice of the priest, who approached the dining room and
whom I would have to tell about my nocturnal visits to the house of
Don Paco, the inventor, my neighbor on the floor below, and of that
diabolical machine that I had secretly learned to operate, and above
all, of my sublime decision which would shock them. I approached
the door and I heard them speaking to my father and my aunt and I
became nervous and my heart began to palpitate and I felt faint and
when Don Claudio and the priest were about to enter, I collapsed on
the sofa. . .   [*She has done and said everything that her dialogue
indicates and she collapses. Felisa enters surreptitiously through the
office door and, upon seeing Florita unconscious, she takes the cognac
bottle from the bureau and exits happily by the door she entered, while
the murmur of the conversation of those about to enter is heard and the
volume of the music increases.*]

CURTAIN

ACT TWO

A Ministry Office. A main door, upstage right; another on the right wall that connects to other offices. On the left wall, a small wooden window which, when opened, reveals an opening through which characters will occasionally speak with an invisible public. Four tables or desks on which are documents, papers, and folders; shelves and bookcases full of the same kinds of papers.

Books and official bulletins on the floor. Everything is dirty, dusty, and in disarray. The room is illuminated by a small, high window upstage left. It's 12:00 noon.

As the curtain opens, we see Hernández, whom we saw walking down the street in the first act; he is a sixty-year-old functionary who occupies the table next to the little window. He is dirty and slovenly looking, wears oversleeves, and is having coffee with half a piece of toast; he wipes off the grease and the coffee that dribble on his chin with an envelope or document. At the same time, he speaks with Ramón, whom we also saw walking down the street in the first act. Ramón is about the same age and state of filth. He wears an orderly's uniform and is resentfully cleaning a table with a feather duster.

RAMÓN   Well, I've heard she's blond, Señor Hernández...

HERNÁNDEZ   [*Astonished.*]   Are you sure, Ramón? That can't be true!...

RAMÓN   It's true...blond!

HERNÁNDEZ   [*Indignant.*]   But that's totally improper! My wife didn't sleep all night long, just thinking that I'm going to have a woman working beside me...because you know me, Ramón, and you know what happened to me on the day of the masked ball.

RAMÓN   [*He stops cleaning and approaches Hernández.*]   Of course I know...they surprised you pinching that woman from Galicia on the arm...

HERNÁNDEZ   Exactly...that's the way it was...it was just that way. She was going up the stairs, dressed as a Galician, and I was behind her; and I got up my courage and said, "What a Galician!"*

RAMÓN   "What a Galician?"

HERNÁNDEZ   That's right! "What a Galician," and I pinched her...

RAMÓN   You really have a way with women, Señor Hernández!

HERNÁNDEZ   I just can't help it...after all, I'm a real man...And you must understand, Ramón, that with this reputation, when my wife finds out that the woman who's coming here is a blond, the poor

---

*In Spanish "Vaya Gallega" ("What a Galician!") has strong sexual connotations; however, because of Mr. Hernandez's age and obvious lack of experience in such matters, this line becomes quite humorous whenever he uses it.

thing will have a fit... Because the Galician was blond...

RAMON   Well, that's what they say at the market... that she's blond... and I mean *blond* blond...

HERNÁNDEZ   This is outrageous! They're going to send us an Apache!   [*There are timid knocks on the window next to Hernández.*]

RAMÓN   They're knocking at the window, Señor Hernández.

HERNÁNDEZ   You think I don't hear?

RAMÓN   They've knocked several times and it is time.

HERNÁNDEZ   It may be time for them, but it's not for me...   [*Very angrily, he opens the window and speaks to someone outside.*]   What's the matter with you, what do you want? Why don't you bang on your head instead of banging on the window? Yes. Of course this is the Ministry of Development. Didn't you see the sign as you came in? Yes, and this is the Office of Public Works. But it's not time, do you understand?... And even if it were, I'm busy. Can't you see that? So just be quiet!   [*And he slams the window shut and continues having breakfast.*]   What a disagreeable sort!

RAMÓN   What an imbecile!   [*Hernández wipes the grease off his chin with an envelope.*]   Would you like for me to give you the newspaper to use instead of today's mail?

HERNÁNDEZ   No. I haven't read the newspaper yet. Besides, no one's going to read the mail...

RAMÓN   [*Taking a seat next to Hernández in a chair that is next to the table.*]   Well, my wife is also a little jealous, Señor Hernández...

HERNÁNDEZ   As well she should be, Ramón. After all, we are men and have blood in our veins, and we come here to work and not to fiddle around... And if that blond comes, I assure you we'll be fiddling around.

RAMÓN   That's what my wife said. But since she kept harping on it, I finally gave her a cuff that put her in bed.

HERNÁNDEZ   And I did the same to mine. It's all right for me to think that, but for women to have an opinion about it is another matter. I'll bet you can't guess what I told her after I slapped her? I'll bet you can't.

RAMÓN   It must have been good. What did you say, Señor Hernández?

HERNÁNDEZ   Well, I said, "Get in the kitchen! Make me some meatballs!"

RAMÓN   Well done, Señor.

HERNÁNDEZ   And I've had her in the kitchen making meatballs since the night before last.   [*Someone knocks at the window again and Hernández opens it once more and confronts the invisible person.*]   Are you knocking again? Yes, sir. This is where you get the papers but it's past the time to hand them out. What did you say? Do you want me to come out there and knock some sense into you? Well, come back tomorrow if you want to! [*He slams the window shut again.*] I'm really not in any mood to put up with this public!... And all because of that Don Claudio, God bless him, who's going to get us in a real mess just because of that floozy. Because she must be one, Ramón. I know what life is all about...

RAMÓN   Well, of course! And this thing is so important to him that he had me clean and straighten the office from top to bottom...

HERNÁNDEZ   [*Looking around at the total disarray of the office.*]   Yes, well, I can see that...it's starting to look effeminate! But you know what I'm thinking, Ramón?

RAMÓN   I can just imagine. What are you thinking?

HERNÁNDEZ   Well, I'm thinking that it's time Don Claudio heard me on this subject! [*Don Claudio's coughing is heard offstage. Ramón gets up.*]

RAMÓN   In fact, he is going to hear you! [*Don Claudio enters through the upstage door. He's a seventy-year-old gentleman with a beard, moustache, glasses, and a cane. He's grave and serious and from time to time has terrible coughing attacks. He's bundled up, with a bowler hat pulled down to his eyebrows and a scarf up to his nose. In his presence, Ramón and Hernández change their attitudes and become respectful and obsequious.*]

DON CLAUDIO   Good morning, gentlemen.

RAMÓN   Good morning, Don Claudio.

HERNÁNDEZ   Don Claudio, good morning. [*As he speaks, Don Claudio slowly takes off his coat, his hat, his scarf and overshoes, helped by Ramón and Hernández, who have solicitously stood up. Don Claudio has another coughing attack.*]

RAMÓN   Seems you've gotten up very early today, Don Claudio!

HERNÁNDEZ   That's true, Don Claudio. It's not yet twelve...

DON CLAUDIO   The fact is I'm a little behind in my work and, besides, since it's such a nice sunny day, I went out on the street to take in a little air...

RAMÓN   Of course, Don Claudio, it's a spring morning...

DON CLAUDIO   So much so that when I left the house, I wondered whether I should put on my overshoes or not. But I put them on just in case.

HERNÁNDEZ   You did the right thing, Don Claudio. One must be careful, it's still July... [*Don Claudio, who has taken his place at the desk downstage right, has a horrible coughing fit. When it has passed, Ramón says to him:*]

RAMÓN   Your cough seems better today...

DON CLAUDIO   It is. I've got some new medicine, and it's working quite

well. [*Coughs again.*]   However, this room is rather cool.   [*To
Ramón.*]   You need to put a little coal on the fire, Ramón...

RAMÓN   You have it locked in your desk drawer. And the coal scoop,
too.   [*Don Claudio takes out a keyring while he speaks. Hernández
has returned to his desk and begun to read the newspaper.*]

DON CLAUDIO   That's true, Ramón! That's true...just think, we have to
hide the coal so the employees don't cart it off...

HERNÁNDEZ   And if it were just the coal! What about the ashes?...
[*Ramón removes some coal from one of Claudio's desk drawers, puts it
in the shovel and then in the stove.*]   And the letter sealers?

RAMÓN   And the window shades?

DON CLAUDIO   And the doorknobs?   [*He continues speaking while he puts
on the black oversleeves of an office clerk.*]   According to the latest sta-
tistics, state employees eat up more than 800 thousand pesetas a year
in letter sealant and as much again in pencil wood. And what they say
is, "As long as they give free bicarbonate of soda in the cafes!" That's
how Spain is going, Señor Hernández...Bicarbonated!

HERNÁNDEZ   You said it, Don Claudio. Bicarbonated and sodiated!

DON CLAUDIO   [*Enigmatically.*]   At least things are at the point of
changing and new times await us.

HERNÁNDEZ   [*Exchanging a glance with Ramón.*]   What are you saying, Don Claudio?

DON CLAUDIO   Nothing...it's not important...have you put everything
in order, Ramón?...

RAMÓN   Yes, sir, as you can see...

DON CLAUDIO   That's true. Everything looks different.   [*He arranges a
few papers that are on the desk.*]   Well, let's begin to work. Are my
things ready, Ramón?   [*Ramón places an open newspaper on his desk
which contains the things he mentions.*]

RAMÓN   Here you are, Don Claudio. Your tobacco, the cigarette paper,
and the tray...

DON CLAUDIO   Thank you, Ramón. Now go see the Undersecretary and
find out if he's fixed the dining room clock that I brought him yesterday.

RAMÓN   Yes, sir...right away...   [*Ramón exits stage right.*]

DON CLAUDIO   All right! Now let's see if I can roll this tobacco!

HERNÁNDEZ   You shouldn't work so hard, Don Claudio.

DON CLAUDIO   It can't be helped, Señor Hernández. Thanks to my abil-
ity to roll cigarettes, I've become the head of the office, which at my
age is quite a promotion. I can't let the Director General down, so I
need to roll at least a box every day.

HERNÁNDEZ   [*Trying to compliment him.*]   I've heard that you're even
going to roll them for the Minister...

DON CLAUDIO [*Modestly lowering his glance.*] Ah! Rumors, just rumors. I have so much yet to learn before that happens!... However, if the Lord gives me health and good fortune... [*Pablo Meléndez, whom we already know, enters through the upstage door. Here, however, he seems timid and servile, wears a different suit, which is more worn and dirtier than the one he wore in the first act.*]

PABLO Good morning, Don Claudio...I'm sorry I'm late, but I was held up in the shoe store...

DON CLAUDIO Then you took my boots in to be fixed, Pablo?

PABLO Yes, sir. And I explained to them how you wanted the half-soles done...but there were so many people...

DON CLAUDIO All right, don't worry, sit down at your desk...

PABLO Yes, sir. [*He goes toward his desk.*] Good morning, Señor Hernández.

HERNÁNDEZ Good morning, Pablito. [*Pablo sits at his desk upstage right. Don Claudio moves the tobacco aside, coughs, and says gravely:*]

DON CLAUDIO Are you seated?

PABLO [*Surprised, as is Hernández.*] Yes, sir.

DON CLAUDIO Well, then...I was only waiting for your arrival so that, once we were all here, I could confirm the grave news which I suppose you already have some knowledge of.

HERNÁNDEZ I've heard something mentioned...

PABLO I've heard some rumors...

HERNÁNDEZ But with all due respect, Don Claudio, I believe that what I've heard can't be true...

DON CLAUDIO Well, it's true, my friends. For the first time in Spain, and I believe the world, a woman is going to come to work in an office. But not as a cleaning woman, which would make sense; rather, as a functionary of public works...

HERNÁNDEZ [*Not believing what he hears.*] As a functionary of public works?

DON CLAUDIO Yes, sir. Just as we are.

PABLO [*Stupified.*] But that's impossible!

HERNÁNDEZ A woman functionary? But what function can a woman have? Can women function outside their homes?...What country are we living in, Don Claudio?

DON CLAUDIO [*He rises and goes centerstage.*] Permit me to finish! This young woman, who is a friend of mine, comes on a probationary basis and I'm sure will not last long among us.

HERNÁNDEZ [*Indignant.*] How could she last? Don't you understand that a woman could never co-exist with persons of the opposite sex without causing serious conflicts of moral and public order?

PABLO   And above all, Don Claudio, she's taking the place of a man who must feed a family...

HERNÁNDEZ   [*Furious.*]   And that's not right!

DON CLAUDIO   Will you let me continue?...

HERNÁNDEZ   Yes, sir, go on...

DON CLAUDIO   The young woman in question is the daughter of a retired official who doesn't have a cent, and she wants this job to earn an honest living and thus feed her family...

HERNÁNDEZ   Well, let her get married...

DON CLAUDIO   She doesn't have a suitor...

HERNÁNDEZ   Well, let her find one!

DON CLAUDIO   She can't.

HERNÁNDEZ   Well, let her die!

DON CLAUDIO   She doesn't want to die!

HERNÁNDEZ   All right, all right; go on, then.

DON CLAUDIO   Some time ago, she called me and a priest together and said to us: "I want to be a public works functionary, just as you are, and earn my living and support my family...and if you don't help me do this, you cause me to become a 'fallen woman'."

HERNÁNDEZ   A fallen woman?

DON CLAUDIO   A fallen woman!

HERNÁNDEZ   That's very serious...

DON CLAUDIO   Imagine our surprise and indignation. We told her she was crazy, and we left her there crying. However, the priest felt remorse and thought it over. He spoke to the Monsignor about the case. The Monsignor spoke to the Bishop...the Bishop to the Minister, and the Minister to our Director General. And unfortunately, the idea was accepted and today, that young woman will come to work in our office...   [*And he returns to his place at his desk.*]

HERNÁNDEZ   Today?

PABLO   [*He straightens his tie.*]   Today?

DON CLAUDIO   Today! However, I want you to know something. Although she and her family are friends of mine, I was the first to oppose this because I think it is shameful and immoral and if this succeeds, life will get more and more difficult...

HERNÁNDEZ   Well, naturally!

PABLO   Of course!

DON CLAUDIO   But I also want you to know that our Director General, who is a man of advanced ideas and who was once in London, is the one most concerned that this work out. And that the gadget also work out...

PABLO   [*Not understanding.*]   The gadget?

HERNÁNDEZ   [*Not understanding either.*]   What gadget?

DON CLAUDIO   The young woman's gadget...because the young woman who is going to come has a gadget...   [*Ramón enters stage right with a dining room clock, which he gives to Don Claudio.*]

RAMÓN   Here's your clock. It's all fixed.

DON CLAUDIO   Ah, very good! Many thanks!...   [*He puts it on the table.*]

RAMÓN   Oh, and the Director asks that you go see him immediately...

DON CLAUDIO   [*Rising.*]   My goodness! I wonder what he wants?

RAMÓN   That's all he said. And that it's urgent.

DON CLAUDIO   I'm going, I'm going right away.   [*Very nervous.*]   Perhaps the silver cigar case I fixed for him yesterday is broken again...   [*He exits stage right.*]

HERNÁNDEZ   [*Rising.*]   Did you hear, Pablito?

PABLO   But how awful!

HERNÁNDEZ   You don't know what you've missed, Ramón.

RAMÓN   Did he tell you anything?

PABLO   Everything.

RAMÓN   But what did he say?

HERNÁNDEZ   That the young woman who's coming has the blessing of the Minister and the Monsignor...

RAMÓN   Good heavens!

HERNÁNDEZ   And also that she's tied in with the Director General.

RAMÓN   I'd already figured that out.

PABLO   Does anyone know what she's like?

HERNÁNDEZ   The young woman?

PABLO   Yes.

RAMÓN   She's blond.

PABLO   That's not possible!

HERNÁNDEZ   Yes she is. And that's not the worst part, Ramón. She's bringing a gadget...

RAMÓN   What gadget?

PABLO   We don't know. Some gadget.

RAMÓN   On a stand?

HERNÁNDEZ   Who knows. What the Director wants is for the gadget to work...   [*The upstage door opens and Florita appears, followed by Don José and Doña Matilde. She has a package in her hand.*]

FLORITA   May I come in?...Good morning.

RAMÓN   Good morning.

DON JOSÉ   Good morning.

MATILDE   Good morning.

HERNÁNDEZ   [*Hernández and Ramón look at the new arrivals with suspicion and antipathy and then take their places. Pablo, who recognizes*

Florita and her family, is disconcerted and then goes to his table, trying to hide his face. Florita goes to Ramón and speaks to him ingenuously and sweetly, trying to be as pleasant as possible, as are Don José and Matilde when their turn arrives. Hernández is very bothered that they go to Ramón and not to him.]

FLORITA   Don Claudio López, is this the place?

RAMÓN   [*Dryly.*]   Yes, this is the place...

FLORITA   Well, I don't see him.

RAMÓN   He's not here.

FLORITA   That's what I thought! Will he be long?

RAMÓN   We don't know. The Director General has asked to see him.

FLORITA   May we wait until he returns?

RAMÓN   As far as I'm concerned, you can.

FLORITA   Thank you very much...I'm the young woman who's coming to work here.

MATILDE   And I'm her aunt.

DON JOSÉ   And I'm her father.

MATILDE   We've left her sister and the maid in the hallway.

DON JOSÉ   In case they'd be a bother, you know?   [*Hernández cannot contain his indignation and says aggressively:*]

HERNÁNDEZ   They probably would be! Because in case you don't know it, that man is the orderly, and I'm the first official and my name is Señor Hernández: Justo Hernández.

FLORITA   Pleased to meet you...

HERNÁNDEZ   Justo Hernández de la Barquera.

FLORITA   Then I'm really pleased to meet you.

DON JOSÉ   Glad to know you.

MATILDE   You seem like such a nice, agreeable person.

HERNÁNDEZ   Well, I'm not, Señora!...

MATILDE   That's too bad, because you look like you could be.

DON JOSÉ   Naturally, if you wanted to...

HERNÁNDEZ   But I don't want to!

FLORITA   Well, if I were you, with those advantages...

HERNÁNDEZ   All right, enough! Go notify Don Claudio, Ramón, and tell him what's happening.

RAMÓN   Yes, Señor Hernández, right away...   [*He exits stage right. Doña Matilde sees Pablo and says to Florita in a low voice:*]

MATILDE   We already know that one, don't we, Florita?   [*Florita realizes the bad time Pablo is having and tries to help him out.*]

FLORITA   I don't remember...

PABLO   [*He rises timidly and approaches them.*]   Yes, I believe I had the pleasure on a certain occasion...

DON JOSÉ   Of course we never saw hide nor hair of you again, neither you nor your friend.

MATILDE   Did he perhaps find another hat that he liked better?

FLORITA   Quiet, Aunt. We need to forget that...

DON JOSÉ   What happened to your millions? Did you lose them in Monte Carlo?

HERNÁNDEZ   [*Not understanding anything of this conversation.*]   What is all this about this young man? You explain it to me, Pablito. What millions are they talking about?

FLORITA   [*She approaches Hernández and lies.*]   Excuse us, Señor Hernández...but my family is confusing him with someone else... that's how absent-minded they are...   [*She looks at Pablo, who acknowledges her intervention with a glance.*]   I would have preferred to come alone but they insisted...

MATILDE   We thought that, the first day...

DON JOSÉ   Besides, if we can help in some way...

MATILDE   That's why we have the maid in the hallway with a broom...

DON JOSÉ   [*In a dramatic tone.*]   You know what a daughter is to a father...and I've been an employee, and I also know what you must think of the intrusion of a woman here. What a scandal! True?

FLORITA   But, Papa!

DON JOSÉ   Quiet! May I?   [*He sits next to Hernández's desk.*]   I cried a lot, Señor Hernández, before giving my consent...I've cried and kicked and moaned, but things were presented in such a way that I had no choice but to give in.   [*He sputters sulkily.*]   How shameful!

MATILDE   [*Sputters also.*]   Just imagine, our neighbors won't even speak to us...

DON JOSÉ   A young woman working as if she were a laborer!...

FLORITA   Come on, Papa! Let's not go back over that...   [*Someone knocks at the little window. Hernández speaks to the family.*]

HERNÁNDEZ   Just a moment.   [*He opens the little window and speaks furiously to the person we suppose has knocked.*]   Just what is the matter with you? Yes, sir. This is where you get those documents. But it's not time to get those documents. No, sir! The correct time is when we have closed! Don't you understand? Well, you're an idiot. Yes, sir! And you're speaking to a functionary who sends you straight to hell!   [*He slams the window.*]

MATILDE   Isn't that something! What you have to put up with...

HERNÁNDEZ   [*He begins to feel less threatened by the family.*]   You just don't know, Señora.

FLORITA   I don't know how you have the patience to be so nice to them...

DON JOSÉ   When I was a functionary, I always had my cane within reach. And the first one who stuck his head in, bam! I hit him with the cane!

That way I didn't even have to speak.

MATILDE   Why don't you lend this gentleman your cane?

DON JOSÉ   Well, if you need it...

HERNÁNDEZ   Thank you very much. That's very kind.   [*Don Claudio enters stage right, followed by Ramón. Don Claudio appears warm and paternal.*]

DON CLAUDIO   Good morning!

FLORITA   Don Claudio!

DON JOSÉ   Señor López!

MATILDE   Señor López!

DON CLAUDIO   But why have you all come? For goodness sakes, for goodness sakes!...

FLORITA   I didn't want them to, but they insisted...

MATILDE   You must understand what this means to us...

DON CLAUDIO   Come, come, you needn't worry, nothing will happen. Everything will be all right, my dear. Have you met these gentlemen?

FLORITA   Yes, we've been introduced.

DON CLAUDIO   Well, then, let's get to work.   [*To Don José and Doña Matilde.*]   And I beg you to leave now, because you cannot all stay here.

MATILDE   [*Almost crying.*]   It's so hard for me to leave my niece...

FLORITA   Couldn't she sit on a chair at my side?

DON CLAUDIO   No, no, absolutely not. Come, Doña Matilde, you may wait, if you want, in the hallway but not here, because it's prohibited...

DON JOSÉ   And when will she be through, more or less?

DON CLAUDIO   At 1:00, just like the rest of us.

MATILDE   [*Referring to the package.*]   I brought her a little lunch...

FLORITA   Please, Aunt, I don't want any. You're going to end up making these gentlemen mad.

DON JOSÉ   [*With dramatic decisiveness.*]   Yes, Matilde. It's best for us to wait outside. Good-bye, dear daughter. A hug.   [*He hugs her emotionally, then shakes hands with Hernández.*]   Good-bye, Señor de la Barquera. And I beg you, please, not to say anything off-color...

FLORITA   [*Hugging them both.*]   Good-bye, Papa. Good-bye, Aunt.

MATILDE   Good-bye, Florita.

DON JOSÉ   [*Gives Don Claudio a hug.*]   Don Claudio!...

DON CLAUDIO   [*To Ramón.*]   You see them out, Ramón, and give them a glass of water for their nerves.

RAMÓN   Yes, Don Claudio...

MATILDE   Good day, gentlemen, and forgive us.

DON JOSÉ   Good day, gentlemen, and you, Florita, don't ever forget that your father was always an honorable man... [*They exit, disconsolate, through the upstage door, followed by Ramón. Florita is left standing centerstage. There's an awkward moment for everyone.*]

DON CLAUDIO   Well, Florita, now we have you here. That is your desk. You may sit down.

FLORITA   Thank you, Don Claudio. [*And Florita sits at the desk indicated, which is upstage center.*]

DON CLAUDIO   You're welcome, Florita, you're welcome. [*Don Claudio, Pablo, and Hernández look at her surreptitiously, as if she were some strange bird, without knowing what to do or say. It's obvious the presence of a woman bothers them. Florita is also inhibited. To break the spell, Don Claudio says to Florita:*] Would you like a cup of coffee?

FLORITA   No, no, thank you very much.

DON CLAUDIO   [*After another awkward pause.*] Have you brought something to sew?

FLORITA   No, sir, I brought nothing... [*Hernández goes to the stove from where he can see Florita better.*]

DON CLAUDIO   [*After coughing a little.*] Well, the Director General, who is a very cultured man and who has traveled abroad a great deal, is quite interested that this experiment work well; and he'll call you later to meet you.

FLORITA   Yes, sir. Thank you very much. [*Since the awkward situation seems to continue, Florita decides to speak.*] Very well, Don Claudio. You must tell me what I have to do.

DON CLAUDIO   [*Puzzled.*] What you have to do? [*Suddenly he remembers that Florita has come to work.*] Of course! Let's see... [*He doesn't know what work to give her.*] Señor Hernández, have you finished addressing the envelopes that I gave you the day before yesterday?

HERNÁNDEZ   [*Surprised by the question.*] How could I have finished when you gave me fourteen? I still have six left.

DON CLAUDIO   Of course, of course...I'm sorry...you're right. [*Suddenly he has an idea.*] Well, in that case, it's all resolved: give this young woman the list with the addresses and some envelopes...

HERNÁNDEZ   The list with addresses and some envelopes?

DON CLAUDIO   Yes, exactly.

HERNÁNDEZ   All right...whatever you want... [*Hernández begins to look among all the papers on his desk for the items requested.*]

DON CLAUDIO   [*Disturbed.*] Can't you find them?

HERNÁNDEZ   [*After looking again.*] Ah! We're in luck! Here's the list! And some envelopes! [*Florita goes to get both.*]

FLORITA Thank you very much...

DON CLAUDIO Come here, Florita. [*He explains everything to her meticulously, as if it were a difficult experiment.*] See here, you have to put these six names and addresses on these envelopes. The city to which they're addressed goes on the lower portion, in larger letters. But don't get nervous, you see. Be calm. You have all morning and afternoon to do it. On your table you will find a quill and inkwell...

FLORITA [*Smiling proudly.*] I don't need them. I've brought an "endless pen."

DON CLAUDIO A what?

FLORITA An endless pen. Look at it. [*Florita removes from her pocket one of the first fountain pens. Pablo and Hernández approach her to look at the pen.*]

DON CLAUDIO And what is that?

FLORITA You remember, my neighbor on the floor below is an inventor and he corresponds with other inventors from America...

DON CLAUDIO Oh, yes!...the one with the gadget...

FLORITA The same one, yes sir. This is a new pen that has ink inside it so you don't have to dip it. He's lent it to me... [*Hernández takes the pen carefullly.*]

HERNÁNDEZ Let's see, you say the ink is inside?

FLORITA Yes, sir... [*To Don Claudio.*] Try it, Don Claudio...you'll see... [*Hernández gives him the pen.*]

DON CLAUDIO Let me see. [*He tries to write on a piece of paper.*] It doesn't write anything.

FLORITA Let me have it. [*She takes it and shakes it several times.*] Because it's a modern invention, you have to do this to it.

DON CLAUDIO [*Not understanding.*] Oh! Of course!

HERNÁNDEZ But do you have to do that to it a lot?

FLORITA Yes, quite a bit. Until the ink drips to the floor.

DON CLAUDIO And do you then pick it up?

FLORITA No, it just stays there. [*She stops shaking the pen.*] It's ready. Write something now...

DON CLAUDIO [*Writing.*] It's true. It does write...and the other gadget you mentioned to me?

FLORITA It's not a gadget, it's a machine that's also used for writing, but in printed letters. You hit on some buttons and it comes out written. Don Paco, my neighbor, has copied it from some of the first ones made by the Americans. I learned to operate it at night, when everyone was asleep and couldn't see me, because the inventor said it was a secret. But now he says it's no longer a secret, that it's patented, and that he'll let me bring it here.

DON CLAUDIO [*Not understanding anything either.*] Of course, of course. . . I suppose it's not dangerous?

FLORITA   No, Señor, not at all!. . .

DON CLAUDIO   I wouldn't want you to cut your finger.

FLORITA   No, Señor. . .it doesn't cut!

DON CLAUDIO   Well, go on, then. Start addressing those envelopes and see how they come out, eh?. . .

FLORITA   Yes, sir.   [*Florita goes to her desk, and Pablo and Hernández, who were standing at her side listening to the business about the machine, do the same. Florita starts writing rapidly. Everyone observes her with curiosity and then Florita gives a happy cry.*]   I've done the envelopes!   [*The three office workers are stupified.*]

DON CLAUDIO   What are you saying, Florita?

FLORITA   That I've finished the envelopes.

DON CLAUDIO   That can't be. . .let's see. . .let's see. . .   [*Florita rises and hands them to him. Don Claudio looks at them one by one.*]   Yes, it's true. And with very neat letters. Show them to Señor Hernández.

FLORITA   Yes, sir.   [*She goes to Señor Hernández' desk and shows them to him.*]

HERNÁNDEZ   Let's see. Actually, they're very well done. And you also wrote them very quickly.

FLORITA   Oh, no! I'm not very good at writing envelopes. . .

DON CLAUDIO   Congratulations, Florita, congratulations. Very good, very good, very good. . .

FLORITA   Thank you very much, Don Claudio.   [*She returns to her desk. But since no one gives her anything to do, she rises and goes to Don Claudio's desk.*]   Very well. . .and what do I do now?

DON CLAUDIO   [*Getting up nervously.*]   Now? Well, right now I'm going to see the Director General to tell him that you're here. Meanwhile, Señor Hernández will tell you what you have to do. . .

FLORITA   Yes, of course. I don't want to be here without doing anything. . .

HERNÁNDEZ   [*Frightened.*]   Me? You want me to tell her?. . .

DON CLAUDIO   Yes. You! Don't you know how to tell a young woman what to do? Aren't you the officer in charge?

HERNÁNDEZ   Yes, sir. . .but that's not. . .

DON CLAUDIO   I'll be right back. Until later, Florita. . .   [*After breathing a sigh of relief because he's found an excuse to free himself from Florita, he exits stage right.*]

FLORITA   All right, Señor Hernández. What should I do now?

HERNÁNDEZ   Well. . .let me think for a minute to see if I can come up with some work to give you. . .what are you doing, Pablito?

PABLO   Multiplication.

HERNÁNDEZ   The problem you can't get right?

PABLO   It's very difficult.

HERNÁNDEZ   Well, perhaps this young woman, who's so smart. . .

FLORITA   Yes, let me see it. . .

PABLO   This is not woman's work. . .

FLORITA   Who knows? Maybe I can get it right. . .

PABLO   In no way. Don't bother.

HERNÁNDEZ   Give it to her, Pablo. That way we'll find out. And you, meanwhile, start opening the mail. . .

PABLO   Yes, sir, whatever you say.   [*He gives her the piece of paper with the multiplication.*]   Here, Señorita; and I'm very sorry.

FLORITA   Don't worry, Pablo. . .

HERNÁNDEZ   You can take all the time you want, Señorita. We're in no hurry.

FLORITA   Yes, sir.   [*Florita begins to work at her desk while Pablo, from his desk, looks at her with pity; Señor Hernández begins to read the newspaper. Florita, very happy, gives another cry.*]   All right! I've got it!

HERNÁNDEZ   [*Almost falling off his chair from shock.*]   You've got it?

FLORITA   Yes, I've multiplied it and I've double-checked it. Look! [*Florita goes to him and shows him.*]

HERNÁNDEZ   You've checked it? Why?

FLORITA   I've even double-checked it, see?

HERNÁNDEZ   Of course. And here's the proof. . . This is very good. Go on back to your desk while I look at it!. . .

FLORITA   [*Doing what she's told.*]   Yes, sir.

HERNÁNDEZ   Look at this, Pablito. See how well she has done it, with the proof and everything?

PABLO   It's extraordinary! What talent!

HERNÁNDEZ   Very good, Señorita. We're quite pleased with you. Now, rest a little, while I read the newspaper. . .   [*Hernández starts reading the newspaper, and Pablo begins to open a letter. But Florita is unable to do nothing and returns to Hernández's desk.*]

FLORITA   But Señor Hernandez, while you're reading the newspaper, what should I be doing?

HERNÁNDEZ   [*Beginning to be irritated, he throws down the newspaper, rises, tries to remain calm.*]   Pablo, what are you doing?

PABLO   The mail. I've opened the letter.

HERNÁNDEZ   There's only one?

PABLO   Yes, sir.

HERNÁNDEZ   Well, seal it up again and that way you won't be through.

FLORITA   [*Still standing behind Hernández.*]   And so. . . tell me what I should do next?

HERNÁNDEZ   Why don't you go out in the hallway for a bit and calm down your family?

FLORITA   No. They will just have to be calm by themselves. [*Hernández has a wonderful idea to free himself of her.*]

HERNÁNDEZ   Water! Why don't you go get a drink of water?

FLORITA   How silly! But I'm not thirsty!

HERNÁNDEZ   [*Now furious.*]   Silly? All right! Well, even though you're not thirsty, you can just go get a drink of water at the fountain and stay in the hallway a bit with your aunt! Understand?

FLORITA   Of course, Señor. As you wish . . . But if you need me for anything . . .

HERNÁNDEZ   We don't need you for anything!

FLORITA   All right, I'll be right back . . .

HERNÁNDEZ   Don't be right back!

FLORITA   Well, then, until later . . .

HERNÁNDEZ   Until much later!

FLORITA   Yes, sir . . . I'll be back.   [*She exits upstage. Hernández collapses in his chair.*]

HERNÁNDEZ   Did you see that, Pablito? . . .

PABLO   She's amazing! . . . I never thought that multiplication . . .

HERNÁNDEZ   And look at the envelopes. What beautiful handwriting . . .

PABLO   It's true . . . And without any smudges . . .

HERNÁNDEZ   Of course on this one, she spelled Huelva with an H . . . But we can't expect a woman to know how to spell.   [*He gets up.*]   But before she returns, Pablito, look through your desk. Maybe you'll find some overdue bill or something we can give her . . .

PABLO   I've already looked everywhere and I can't find a thing.

HERNÁNDEZ   She's going to think that we don't do anything in this ministry . . .   [*Florita enters upstage, very happy.*]

FLORITA   Señor Hernández, they've left.

HERNÁNDEZ   Who has?

FLORITA   My family. I've convinced them to leave. I'm so excited about going home alone for the first time!

HERNÁNDEZ   Naturally, naturally . . .

FLORITA   All right, and what should I do now? . . .

HERNÁNDEZ   Well, now, precisely . . .   [*Someone knocks at the little window.*]

FLORITA   Would you like for me to open the window? Someone's calling . . .

HERNÁNDEZ   Yes, yes . . . open the window, but close it right away because there's a draft.   [*Florita takes Hernández's place at his desk and opens the window and speaks to the person we assume is on the other side. She's very cordial and helpful.*]

FLORITA   Yes, Señor. How can I help you?...Yes, Señor, this is the office. Yes, of course. I'm employed at the Ministry...Naturally you can say whatever you like. Let's see. Would you be so kind? [*She puts her hand out the window and takes the piece of paper that is handed to her.*] Yes. This is where you present this document. Of course it's the right time, yes sir...But would you please attach the correct seal. Yes. You can get it right down this street. It will be five cents, sir. Not at all. We're here to serve you. Thank you very much, sir.   [*She closes the window. Pablo and Hernández look at each other, amazed at the kind words of Florita. Florita turns and says:*] All right. I've finished with that gentleman. What should I do now?   [*Hernández, like Don Claudio, thinks it best to flee. He picks up a pencil from the table.*]

HERNÁNDEZ   Look here, young lady; I want you to sharpen this pencil while I go find Don Claudio. Do you understand? All right, I'll be right back.   [*He leaves, running through the door to the right. Florita stays at Hernández's table and begins to sharpen the pencil with a little blade. Pablo, who has not ceased looking at her from his desk, decides to speak to her as he approaches.*]

PABLO   Thank you very much, Florita.

FLORITA   [*Surprised.*]   Why are you thanking me?...

PABLO   Because you didn't mention anything in front of my employers. If they should find out about my deception...

FLORITA   That wasn't important, Pablo...

PABLO   Yes, it was...I lied to you...I told you about my father's millions, and you see what I really am...a poor pencil-pusher.

FLORITA   We also lied to you. Neither my sister nor I know how to make sweets, or liqueur, or chairs, and that homey atmosphere, with the cat and everything, isn't real. We spend our life there complaining.

PABLO   But you were lying in order to find a fiancé so you could get married...and we, on the other hand, visit the homes of eligible young women to get something to eat. Because the truth is, we're hungry.

FLORITA   That's true. You ate all the pastries...

PABLO   They were so good, Florita!

FLORITA   They were the most expensive kind. To buy those pastries, we went without dinner. And to buy my sister's hat, my father almost died of starvation.

PABLO   [*Moved.*]   You don't know how sorry I am...

FLORITA   Don't worry. Thanks to those things, and others like them, I'm now here, sharpening a pencil and very happy.

PABLO   Why?

FLORITA   Because in a few years, you'll run out of anisette and pastries, and unless you find a new game like football to enjoy, I don't think you're going to have much entertainment...

PABLO   Florita! I beg you to forgive me!

FLORITA   You're forgiven...And what happened to your friend?

PABLO   Manolo is still in love with Cecilia.

FLORITA   What an original way to be in love! We never saw him after that day.

PABLO   Manolo works in another ministry, and he's as poor as I am. Your father led us to believe that you were very wealthy. And your aunt said that Cecilia had just returned from the home of the Duchess of Montpellier. Just imagine! That made Manolo feel inferior and he didn't return. But I know that he loves her...

FLORITA   And your friend believed all that?

PABLO   Of course...just as I did...

FLORITA   How awful! My poor aunt stages things very well, but I've told her that sometimes she goes overboard...

PABLO   I assure you that Manolo, had it not been for that...because he does love her. And he's looking for a humble young woman like himself...and when we left there that afternoon...

FLORITA   What happened?

PABLO   [*Emotional: he draws closer to her.*]   We were both impressed with your charm and personality. And knew that you were right in what you said. I've thought a lot about you, Florita...That's why, when I saw you here today...I don't know what my heart felt... [*At that moment, Hernández enters stage right with some papers and hears the last words of the dialogue. Without knowing why, he gets irritated and jealous.*]

HERNÁNDEZ   What are you doing there, Pablito?

PABLO   Nothing. I was telling this young woman...

HERNÁNDEZ   You're no one to tell her anything...

PABLO   [*Surprised.*]   I'm not?

HERNÁNDEZ   No, Señor. No, sir! And instead of playing the fool, go get me a cup of coffee.

PABLO   I wasn't playing the fool, Señor Hernández, and we have a janitor to get your coffee.

HERNÁNDEZ   Since when do you speak to me in that tone? What kind of disrespect is this?

PABLO   Well, if I'm just here to run errands...

HERNÁNDEZ   You're here to do whatever your superiors tell you to do and not to speak to that young woman. Do you understand me? So go on! And don't forget that I'm the head of the office and you're the lowest flunky.

PABLO   [*With dignity.*]   I'm a clerk.

HERNÁNDEZ   Be quiet! Go get my coffee and let's end this discussion!... [*Hernández's tone is cutting, and Pablo humbly lowers his head and goes toward the upstage door.*]

PABLO   Yes, sir... [*Pablo exits.*]

HERNÁNDEZ   Isn't that something! [*Hernández approaches Florita and leans on the back of her chair in a friendly manner, as Pablo did before.*] These young men of today!...

FLORITA   [*Somewhat uneasy.*] I'm going to go to my desk, Señor Hernández...

HERNÁNDEZ   Not at all...You're fine right there... [*He draws closer to her, with increasing friendliness and gallantry.*] How are you doing with that pencil?

FLORITA   Well, just so-so... [*And she shows him a very stubby pencil, which is all she has left after she has sharpened it so much.*]

HERNÁNDEZ   What do you mean so-so? You sharpened it very well... And you have very beautiful hands.

FLORITA   Only my little finger.

HERNÁNDEZ   Nonsense; very delicate, white hands...

FLORITA   Thank you very much.

HERNÁNDEZ   [*Insinuating and seductive.*] You're welcome, darling...Do you have a Galician costume?

FLORITA   [*Surprised by the question and the tone.*] No, Señor.

HERNÁNDEZ   What a shame!

FLORITA   Why?

HERNÁNDEZ   Because then, if you dressed up like a Galician, I could say to you, "What a Galician!"

FLORITA   [*Not understanding.*] Of course. And if I dressed as an Asturian?

HERNÁNDEZ   Then I would say, "What a Galician!"

FLORITA   Ah! You always say the same thing?

HERNÁNDEZ   Why should I change it if it worked well once?...

FLORITA   Of course; you're right.

HERNÁNDEZ   Naturally I'm right...I would really like to meet you at a masked ball, dressed in whatever, so I could say to you, "What a Galician!"

FLORITA   Perhaps during Carnival...

HERNÁNDEZ   [*Suggestively, winking at her.*] If God is willing...true?

FLORITA   True; if God is willing... [*Don Claudio enters stage right with a stack of papers under his arm and hears the last words of the dialogue. He reacts in the same way Hernández did before.*]

DON CLAUDIO   What are you doing there, Señor Hernández?

HERNÁNDEZ   I was watching her sharpen a pencil...

DON CLAUDIO   Well, you ought to be working...

HERNÁNDEZ   Working?

DON CLAUDIO   Yes, sir, working. And you, Florita, get up from there and go to your desk.

FLORITA   But Señor Hernández told me. . .

DON CLAUDIO   Señor Hernández has nothing to tell you because I'm the head of this office.

HERNÁNDEZ   I just thought, so as not to bother her. . .

DON CLAUDIO   Be quiet! Go ask the porter to give you *The Globe* because I haven't read it yet.

HERNÁNDEZ   Couldn't you send the janitor?

DON CLAUDIO   The janitor isn't here and I'm sending you. Is there something wrong with that? So go. . .get me *The Globe.*

HERNÁNDEZ   Yes, sir. But really. . .there's no reason for you to get so upset.

DON CLAUDIO   I'll get any way I want to!

HERNÁNDEZ   All right, that's fine.   [*He exits stage right. Don Claudio approaches Florita in a very friendly manner.*]

DON CLAUDIO   These decrepit old men!. . .   [*And he leans on the back of Florita's chair.*]   How are you, Florita?

FLORITA   I'm fine, thank you.

DON CLAUDIO   Are you happy?

FLORITA   Yes, sir, very. . .

DON CLAUDIO   The Director says he will see you tomorrow. . .

FLORITA   Oh, how nice!   [*Don Claudio smoothes his moustache petulantly.*]

DON CLAUDIO   But, naturally, he's given me a free hand in this experiment. Whether you stay here or not depends entirely on me. . .

FLORITA   And how is it going?. . .

DON CLAUDIO   [*Suggestively.*]   It's going exceptionally well. Exceptionally well!   [*Pablo enters upstage with the coffee service and a tray. Don Claudio is mad at being interrupted.*]   What are you doing here, Pablito?

PABLO   I brought the coffee.

DON CLAUDIO   What coffee?

PABLO   The coffee Señor Hernández asked for.

DON CLAUDIO   And just what gives Señor Hernández the right to send you for coffee? Is Señor Hernández in charge here? I'm the only one in charge here!   [*Hernández enters stage right with a copy of* The Globe.]

HERNÁNDEZ   I've asked him to get me coffee before and nothing like this has happened!

DON CLAUDIO   [*Furious.*]   You're no one to ask for anything!

PABLO   [*Also furious.*]   He did it to humiliate me, Don Claudio!

HERNÁNDEZ   [*Also furious.*]   I did it because I damned well felt like it!   [*Florita gets up, frightened, and slowly moves toward the prosce-nium without taking her eyes off them.*]

DON CLAUDIO   I won't tolerate that kind of language!

HERNÁNDEZ   And I won't tolerate your impertinence!

DON CLAUDIO   You're an imbecile!

HERNÁNDEZ   If you weren't the boss, I'd tell you what you are...

PABLO   I'm not the boss, and I'm telling you you're a pig...

HERNÁNDEZ   A pig?

PABLO   And a miserable one at that!

DON CLAUDIO   Silence!

HERNÁNDEZ   He's offending me!

PABLO   I'm telling him the truth!

DON CLAUDIO   I'll decide what the truth is!

PABLO   [*To Hernández.*]   You're taking advantage because you're an old man!

HERNÁNDEZ   An old man?   [*He picks up a pair of scissors from his desk.*]   Would you like for me to cut out your guts?

PABLO   You? My guts?

DON CLAUDIO   Put those scissors down immediately!   [*The curtains close at the end of this discussion and Florita, who was at first terri-fied, now smiles, leaning on the proscenium in front of the curtains and looking towards the audience as if remembering something. When the background music begins, she speaks in the evocative tone she used in the first act.*]

FLORITA   I remember how that argument, which began so suddenly, without any reason, surprised and worried me...Why did those gentlemen, who had at first received me so curtly, why did they later want to be alone with me and to be so friendly? And why did they suddenly say such vulgar things to each other and want to kill each other with those scissors? Even Don Claudio, such a good friend of the family and so old, why did he look at me in an insinuating man-ner and even seem to cough less? Is it that the presence of a woman in that somber cave had awakened amorous instincts that they thought were asleep? But I had done nothing to awaken them... Besides, no one had ever found me appealing. On the other hand, Pablo himself had appealed to me enormously the first day I saw him at my house; maybe that's why I said so many cruel things to him...and later, in the office, when I saw him so humble, I liked him a great deal...Anyhow, calm was finally restored and the following day I went back with my writing machine, which amazed them, and I was very happy with my work and my colleagues were very amia-ble and it even seemed that they were cleaner than they were the first time I saw them and that they worked harder. Until one day...

That day when I arrived at my desk at nine on the dot, as I usually did, it was already warm and so I took off my jacket. [*Florita has taken off her jacket, which reveals more of her low-necked dress. The curtains have opened and we see that everything is more orderly than it was before and that there is a flower on every desk. On Florita's desk is a large artifact, the writing machine. Ramón, the janitor, is cleaner; he is brushing his uniform and greets Florita warmly when she, from the proscenium, walks toward her desk.*]   Good morning, Ramón.

RAMÓN   Good morning, Señorita Flora...

FLORITA   Beautiful morning, isn't it?

RAMÓN   Yes, Señorita, beautiful morning... [*Florita sits in front of the typewriter and begins to type, making a racket as she hits the keys.*]

FLORITA   All right! I'll see if I can finish up these papers...

RAMÓN   Using that thing, it will be very quick. What an invention, right? It goes so fast! It makes me dizzy sometimes...

FLORITA   [*Typing very slowly.*]   It's all a matter of getting used to it, Ramón. [*Hernández, totally changed, enters upstage. He no longer wears an overcoat; he's wearing a straw hat and has a flower in his lapel. He's very cordial and much cleaner.*]

HERNÁNDEZ   Good morning, my friends...

RAMÓN   Good morning...

FLORITA   Good morning, Señor Hernández.

HERNÁNDEZ   Good morning, Florita.

RAMÓN   [*A little upset because his conversation with Florita was interrupted.*]   You seem to be a little early today...

HERNÁNDEZ   Does it bother you that I arrive at the office on time?

RAMÓN   No, it doesn't bother me...but it surprises me.

HERNÁNDEZ   Well, don't let it surprise you so much and go get me a little coffee...

RAMÓN   A little coffee?

HERNÁNDEZ   Yes. A little coffee. With a little milk...don't you know what a little coffee means?...

RAMÓN   [*Indolently.*]   Yes, sir,... but do I have to go now?...

HERNÁNDEZ   Come on, Ramón. Don't make me lose my patience. And with some toast.

RAMÓN   [*As he exits upstage.*]   Yes, sir...

HERNÁNDEZ   From upstairs.

RAMÓN   Yes, sir. [*Hernández has taken his place next to the little window, has smelled the flowers, has run a comb through his hair and, once Ramón has left, says to Florita:*]

HERNÁNDEZ   Beautiful day, isn't it.

FLORITA   [*She never stops typing.*]   Yes, sir. Very beautiful...

HERNÁNDEZ   On a day like this, it's a pleasure to be alive, isn't it?...

FLORITA   Yes, sir, it certainly is... [*There's knocking at the little window, and Hernández quickly opens it and speaks cordially to someone.*]

HERNÁNDEZ   Good day to you, sir. Yes, sir. Of course...we're all here to serve you. Actually, we now open earlier. Yes, sir...let me see it. [*He takes the document and looks at it.*] Very good. Very good...you already have the stamp and everything is in order. Perfect, perfect...thank you very much, sir...continued health to you, sir. [*He looks through the window to watch him leave.*] No...not that way...through the door to the right...that's correct. You're welcome, sir. Continued health to you, sir. [*He gently closes the window and approaches Florita.*] What a nice man! Wasn't he? Not at all like the people who used to come here!...and you, Florita, today you're prettier than ever...

FLORITA   Am I?

HERNÁNDEZ   But of course...how can I put it...and with the perfume you're wearing... [*Pablo enters upstage. He is also better dressed but within his means. Hernández's presence bothers him a little, and Hernández is also bothered by his interruption.*]

PABLO   Good morning, Florita...

FLORITA   Good morning, Pablo.

PABLO   Good morning, Señor Hernández...

HERNÁNDEZ   You're here already?

PABLO   It's 9:15...

HERNÁNDEZ   You've never been here at 9:15...

PABLO   Neither have you, Señor Hernández...

HERNÁNDEZ   [*Really angry.*] I'm the first official and I come when I feel like it...

PABLO   You have no right to treat me like this.

HERNÁNDEZ   I'll treat you any way I feel like...no more back talk. And go get me the newspaper.

PABLO   Have the janitor get it for you...

HERNÁNDEZ   *You* will get it for me. [*Pablo gets up from his chair and confronts Hernández, ready for anything, while Florita continues her work.*]

PABLO   Well, I don't feel like getting it.

HERNÁNDEZ   You don't feel like it?

PABLO   No, sir. I've had enough of this. I'm tired of your abusiveness, and I'm going to smash your face.

HERNÁNDEZ   You're going to smash my face? [*Ramón enters with the tray and the coffee service.*]

RAMÓN   What's the matter here? You shouldn't be acting this way!

HERNÁNDEZ   [*To Ramón.*]   You can go to the devil!

RAMÓN   To the devil?   [*Don Claudio enters upstage. He's also neater and is not wearing an overcoat. He's heard the last words of the altercation and says, in a cutting and serious voice:*]

DON CLAUDIO   Everyone to their places!

PABLO   But Señor Hernández...

DON CLAUDIO   Quiet! To your places! And silence!

HERNÁNDEZ   [*To Pablo.*]   I'm the first official!

DON CLAUDIO   I said silence!...   [*Everyone takes his place. Don Claudio does also. After a pause he says gravely and with feeling:*] Florita, it's very painful for me to say what I'm going to say to you, but I think the moment has arrived...ever since you have set foot in this office, it has become a battlefield.

FLORITA   But Don Claudio, I haven't done anything!

DON CLAUDIO   I know, Florita, and I don't blame you but rather us, myself included. It's not you...but your presence,...your perfume,...everything that I suspected!...Say what they may in other countries, women will never be able to work beside men. The experiment just hasn't turned out well and I'm the first to lament it. Therefore, there's only one solution left.   [*He lowers his eyes to continue.*]   You must leave...

FLORITA   [*Anguished.*]   But Don Claudio!

PABLO   She's not to blame for anything!...

DON CLAUDIO   You, Pablito, be quiet. And you, Florita, are fired.

FLORITA   [*With tears in her eyes.*]   Then this means...

DON CLAUDIO   [*Also moved.*]   Yes...Gather your things; the sooner you leave, the better. I'll speak with your family and explain it to them. Naturally, I'll be sure they know you're not to blame...   [*Florita rises, picks up her flower vase, and looks lovingly at the typewriter.*]

FLORITA   And my machine?

RAMÓN   I'll bring it to you, Señorita.

FLORITA   Thank you, Ramón.

RAMÓN   Later, at 1:00...when we get off.

FLORITA   Thank you very much.   [*She approaches Don Claudio.*]   Then, Don Claudio, I can't hope that someday...

DON CLAUDIO   No, Florita, you can't hope for anything...I'm very sorry. Good-bye.

FLORITA   Good-bye, Don Claudio. Good-bye, Pablo.

PABLO   [*Emotionally.*]   Good-bye, Florita.

FLORITA   Good-bye, Señor Hernández.

HERNÁNDEZ   [*Also emotionally.*]   Good-bye, Señorita.

FLORITA   Good-bye, Ramón.

RAMÓN   Until later.   [*Florita looks over the room in farewell and, wiping her eyes, exits upstage. Pablo gets up from his chair and goes to the window as if watching her leave. Don Claudio coughs, as always, and puts on his oversleeves. Meanwhile, someone knocks at the little window, and Hernández, with his former bad manners, opens it and yells at the person who has called:*]

HERNÁNDEZ   What's the matter with you? Why don't you find something else to pound on? No, sir. It's not time yet. Do you think that 9:30 is any time for us to be here? Well, no, sir! And don't bother us anymore, you can go to the devil . . . What do they think this is!   [*He slams the window shut and begins to drink the coffee that Ramón has brought him.*]

CURTAIN

ACT THREE

The same set as act 1. It is five in the afternoon; six days have passed since the action in act 2.

The piano is gone and in its place is a table on which sits Florita's typewriter, protected by an oilcloth cover. Because it is warm, the brazier is also gone.

As the curtain rises, a group consisting of Don José, Doña Rosa, Valentina, and Cecilia is seated at the right; Cecilia is sewing on a small piece of cloth. Everyone is quiet, but from Florita's room, we hear Doña Matilde sobbing. Everyone acts as if they don't hear anything. After a few moments, they begin to talk as if continuing an interrupted conversation.

DON JOSÉ   Very well, very well...

DOÑA ROSA   Of course...

VALENTINA   Naturally...

CECILIA   Certainly...

DON JOSÉ   [*To Doña Rosa.*]   Then your father was from Vigo?

DOÑA ROSA   Yes, my father was, but my mother was from Pamplona.

DON JOSÉ   That's much better! Some variety!

CECILIA   And that, in a married couple, must be very entertaining.

VALENTINA   That's just what I say. If they had both been from Vigo, they would always have talked about Vigo.

DON JOSÉ   On the other hand, since she was from Pamplona, they probably only spoke of Pamplona.

CECILIA   And about Vigo, nothing...

DON JOSÉ   Of course...

DOÑA ROSA   Certainly...   [*At that moment, from Florita's room we hear Doña Matilde's voice; she is arguing with her niece.*]

VOICE OF MATILDE   Florita! Have some compassion! I beg of you!...

VOICE OF FLORITA   You need not beg, Aunt. It's useless now.

VOICE OF MATILDE   What you're doing is unforgivable!

VOICE OF FLORITA   And can what they did to me be forgiven?

VOICE OF MATILDE   I've cried and I've implored you! However, my patience has a limit, and since you won't give in, you may do whatever you want, but don't count on your aunt for anything. Good-bye, Florita.

VOICE OF FLORITA   Good-bye, Aunt.   [*The door to the right opens and Doña Matilde leaves the room and slams the door. Without even noticing the visitors, she goes crying to the office door; but being called by Cecilia and seeing the group, she changes her expression, smiles, greets them, and takes a seat as if nothing were wrong.*]

CECILIA   Auntie!

DOÑA MATILDE   Well, how nice! Doña Rosa and Valentina are here! How are you! I haven't seen you for ages...

DOÑA ROSA   As you can see... We've come to visit...

DOÑA MATILDE   Well, how nice. I'm so glad!... And so? What's new?

DOÑA ROSA   Well... nothing. And you?

DOÑA MATILDE   Nothing new, either. [*And everyone smiles violently without knowing what to say, until Valentina decides to speak.*]

VALENTINA   Listen, Doña Matilde, are you having a problem with Florita?

DOÑA MATILDE   [*Feigning astonishment.*]   Us? Oh, no! What kind of a problem could we be having? We're just as happy as ever!

DOÑA ROSA   It's just that we thought we heard something...

VALENTINA   Yes. Something like you crying...

DOÑA ROSA   And then an argument...

DOÑA MATILDE   Ah, well, yes! She was having a snack and didn't want to finish her chocolate because she says she has no appetite...

DOÑA ROSA   [*Sarcastically.*]   Possibly because of her problem...

DOÑA MATILDE   What problem?

VALENTINA   I've heard she's been removed from her job. I mean, that they've thrown her out.

DOÑA MATILDE   [*Laughing.*]   But Cecilia, do you hear?

CECILIA   [*Also laughing.*]   How absurd!

DON JOSÉ   That's totally ridiculous! How could they throw her out when she's the one who does everything in the office?

VALENTINA   Well, that's what they say... That Florita began to flirt with all the functionaries and created a major scandal and that the municipal authorities had to intervene.

DOÑA ROSA   I don't believe it, of course... such a prudent young woman... as prudent as a woman who wants to work in an office can be, of course.   [*All of them speak amiably and kindly, in contrast to the atrocities they are saying.*]

VALENTINA   Prudent and good... Because although Florita can't be said to be pretty, not in the least, she *is* innocent...

DON JOSÉ   You're the innocent ones, allowing yourselves to be deceived like fools... not that it's all your fault, because some people are such good liars and have such evil intentions...

DOÑA MATILDE   The truth is, Florita has been granted a short vacation...

CECILIA   To take a tonic for a few days, because she's a bit weak from working so hard...

VALENTINA   She's always been a little weak, ever since childhood, and because I'm so fond of her... I'm so sorry!

DOÑA MATILDE   You should take a tonic too, Valentina... you're skin and bones.

CECILIA [*Looking at her with pity.*]   It's true...and you used to be so pretty! Poor thing!...

DON JOSÉ   I remember that on the day she was born, she was beautiful, but on the following day, she suffered a big change.

DOÑA ROSA   True; that happened to your daughters also, José. They were born beautiful in the morning, and by nightfall, it was another matter...

DON JOSÉ   Exactly...Those are changes of nature...Moreover, women — as you know from experience — begin to spoil on the sixth day...

DOÑA ROSA   That's true. Cecilia is also quite thin. But that's understandable, since she now has a suitor for the first time...

VALENTINA   You can't imagine how happy I was with the news!... Because I know it's really been difficult for you, dear. You deserve a medal.

DOÑA ROSA   Of course, of course.

CECILIA   By the way, Valentina...You don't know how upset I was when I learned that your father had been put out of office...

DOÑA MATILDE   Yes...What a shame!...And according to the porter, in such sad financial conditions...

DOÑA ROSA   It's not important. During this last crisis, they removed him from office because of the change in government.

DON JOSÉ   I heard they changed the government for just that reason: because they're sick of your husband...Of course I don't believe it for a minute...

CECILIA   The worst thing about it is that your fiancé has abandoned you because of it...

DOÑA MATILDE   That just shows he didn't love you at all but only the money your father had...What a scoundrel!

DON JOSÉ   A rascal!

VALENTINA   Is it true that your suitor's friend, the one who is so ugly, is in love with Florita?

CECILIA   Yes, Pablo Meléndez...he works in her office and has a great future...

DOÑA ROSA   I think, however, he's one of those young men who pretend they want to be married only to come to people's homes to get something to eat.

DOÑA MATILDE   Well, of course in this house we eat so well...

DON JOSÉ   In others, as you must know from experience, Doña Rosa, half a tomato and thanks...

DOÑA ROSA   You're so right...and by the way, I see you don't have the piano here anymore...

DOÑA MATILDE   [*She turns to look at the place where the piano used to be and says, very surprised:*]   Oh, that's true! I hadn't noticed!

DON JOSÉ   Perhaps the maid, while sweeping...

DOÑA MATILDE   They're so scatter-brained...

CECILIA   They never remember where they put things...

VALENTINA   Well, I saw it yesterday in a pawn shop...

DON JOSÉ   But how awful! Where does Felisa have her head?

DOÑA ROSA   [*Rising.*]   Well, we're going to have to go because we still have other visits to make...   [*All of them get up except Don José, who stays in his chair, worried.*]

DOÑA MATILDE   I'm so sorry...

VALENTINA   So are we. We were having such a good time...

CECILIA   You must come more often...

DOÑA MATILDE   Of course...you know how much we enjoy you...

DOÑA ROSA   And we, too. And I'm so happy to hear that the business about Florita was only a rumor and they haven't fired her yet...

VALENTINA   Because when they fire her...what is the poor thing going to do?...

DOÑA ROSA   That's true! With the reputation she has earned with all this business!...Because she does have a reputation...

VALENTINA   Now that no one will speak to her because of that outlandish idea of wanting to work...Anyway, good afternoon and until we see you again...

DOÑA ROSA   Good afternoon...

DOÑA MATILDE   Good afternoon, and I hope you'll come again soon...   [*The four women kiss each other on the cheek very noisily and with much affection.*]

DOÑA ROSA   Good-bye, Don José...Good-bye, Cecilia...

DON JOSÉ   Good-bye, Señora...

VALENTINA   Don't bother seeing us out, Doña Matilde.

DOÑA MATILDE   But of course I will...   [*Doña Matilde, Doña Rosa and Valentina exit through the hallway door, leaving Don José and Cecilia. Don José says dramatically:*]

DON JOSÉ   What a bad time I had! I was afraid they were going to say something rude!

CECILIA   No, Papa...You saw how very affectionate and caring they were...

DON JOSÉ   Yes, that's true.   [*And he continues, still anguished and dramatic.*]   But with this matter of your sister's, I'm always afraid that someone will say something disagreeable...However, this time, at the least suggestion of rudeness, I would have known how to respond in kind...and your aunt would have too, because when she wants to, she can be very frank...

CECILIA   You shouldn't worry. . . Doña Rosa and Valentina really care for us. They are the best friends we have. . .

DON JOSÉ   That's true. . . And we care for them, too, and in these hard times, there's nothing more consoling than having good friends who encourage us with their words. . .

CECILIA   What I don't understand is why you denied the fact that Florita had been fired.

DON JOSÉ   Because with good friends, you have to deny everything and try to keep them from finding out. . . because when they do find out, they move on to other homes to gossip and you never see them again and so you're left bored. . .

CECILIA   And they're so good!. . .

DON JOSÉ   It's true, poor dears. . . Just imagine, the father's been dismissed as a thief!. . . Go on, Cecilia. . . See what your sister is doing. . .

CECILIA   Yes, Papa. . .

DON JOSÉ   But don't go in. . . peek through the keyhole. . .

CECILIA   Yes. . .   [*Cecilia peeks through the keyhole of Florita's room; then she returns sadly to her place.*]

DON JOSÉ   What's she doing?

CECILIA   The same thing. . . She's in front of the mirror smiling.

DON JOSÉ   Horrible! Horrible! Give me my medicine, dear. . .

CECILIA   Don't you feel any better?

DON JOSÉ   I'm feeling worse all the time.   [*Cecilia has gone to the bureau where she gets a spoon and the medicine bottle.*]

CECILIA   There's barely a spoonful left in the bottle. . .

DON JOSÉ   If we just hadn't wasted it on that damned cat! And for all the good the cat did us!

CECILIA   [*She gives Don José the spoon, and he drinks the medicine with pleasure.*]   You shouldn't be unfair. . . since that day, Manolo and Pablo have been in love with us. . .

DON JOSÉ   That's true. . . but how are you going to get ahead with those fellows who earn only fifteen duros* a month?

CECILIA   Manolo says he's going to get a raise. . .

DON JOSÉ   Nonsense! Foolishness!. . . Lies that the government circulates so that women have some illusions and don't strangle their husbands at night. . . Go on, Cecilia. . . Look again to see what your sister is doing. . .

CECILIA   [*Resisting.*]   But Papa. . .

DON JOSÉ   Look, damn it!   [*Cecilia looks through the keyhole again.*]   What?

---

*Spanish coin worth five pesetas.

CECILIA   Just as before, in front of the mirror...but she has one eye closed...

DON JOSÉ   Why should she close one eye! How unfortunate, my God! What have I done to deserve this punishment? I've been an honorable, faithful, and hard-working man...From the time I married your sainted mother, may she rest in peace, I stopped drinking and smoking so as to spend less, I never went out on the streets with my friends. Not because your mother ever said anything, but because she locked the door and hid the key in her garter...I've been happy with my modest life,...and now...What have I done, dear God?   [*He sobs, upset.*]

CECILIA   Calm down, Papa!   [*Doña Matilde enters through the hallway door.*]

DOÑA MATILDE   What's the matter, what's happening now?

CECILIA   Papa's upset...

DOÑA MATILDE   You must have given him his medicine...

DON JOSÉ   I have to get my nourishment somewhere...

DOÑA MATILDE   Have you seen Florita?

CECILIA   She's still in front of the mirror with one eye closed...

DOÑA MATILDE   This is terrible! She's been there since 11:00 this morning and it's now past 5:15...   [*Manolo enters precipitously and nervously through the hallway door.*]

MANOLO   Cecilia!

CECILIA   [*She rises, goes toward him, they shake hands warmly.*] Manolo!

MANOLO   Good afternoon, Don José...good afternoon, Doña Matilde. Please forgive me for not having Felisa announce me, but I'm very nervous...May I sit down?

DON JOSÉ   Yes, of course, sit down.

MANOLO   Thank you...   [*He sits.*]   I hardly ever get nervous, but when I do...May I get up?

DOÑA MATILDE   Yes, Señor...get up...

MANOLO   [*He goes toward Cecilia again.*]   Hello, Cecilia.

CECILIA   Hello, Manolo...

MANOLO   Why aren't you wearing that hat?

CECILIA   Yesterday you told me that you also liked me without it...

DOÑA MATILDE   That's true...I heard you...I hope you're not going to deny it...

DON JOSÉ   You must understand that she doesn't care either way, and if you prefer her with a hat...

MANOLO   I prefer her both ways, but now I want her to put it on because we're going to go out...

CECILIA   We're going out?

DOÑA MATILDE   But what are you saying?. . .

MANOLO   Yes, Señora. . .and you also. . .I have a horse-drawn carriage below.

CECILIA   A carriage?   [*She runs to the balcony and looks out.*]

DOÑA MATILDE   I think you're making fun of us. . .

MANOLO   Yes, yes. . .making fun. . .

CECILIA   [*She returns from the balcony.*]   It's true, Papa! There is a carriage.

DON JOSÉ   Would you like to explain, sir?

MANOLO   Yes, sir. . .May I sit down?

DON JOSÉ   Yes, you may sit down, but you may not get up. . .

MANOLO   Yes, sir. . .   [*He sits.*]   All right, it's very simple. . .The latest change in government has stirred up half the country. But not the other half. . .

DON JOSÉ   And which half are you in?

MANOLO   Which half? But don't you see how nervous I am?. . .In the bad one!

CECILIA   Good Lord!

DOÑA MATILDE   Heavens!

DON JOSÉ   Dismissed!

MANOLO   Until this morning. . .There's been another crisis, the conservatives have gone out, the liberals have come in, and now I'm in the good half. And furthermore, they've raised all of our salaries.

CECILIA   Thank heavens!

DON JOSÉ   No!

MANOLO   Yes. And you know how much?

DON JOSÉ   Some pittance. . .

MANOLO   No, Señor. They've raised it three duros per month!

DOÑA MATILDE   Fifteen pesetas?

DON JOSÉ   Sixty reales*?

MANOLO   Yes. . .Now you will understand my nervous state?. . . Because with this raise, Cecilia and I can get married right away and get our own apartment and live comfortably. And we can even take a long honeymoon. . .Maybe even to Alicante!. . .

DOÑA MATILDE   Naturally! With a raise like that!. . .

MANOLO   That's why, as soon as I heard the news, I went to see the paymaster and asked him to lend me sixty reales and I rented the carriage. And now I want to take you to the best pastry shop in Madrid. . .

DOÑA MATILDE   To eat pastries?

MANOLO   All you want. . .

---

*Spanish coin, no longer in use today, worth twenty-five peseta cents.

DOÑA MATILDE   [*Rising.*]   Let's stop talking...I'll go get ready now
and be right down...   [*She exits very happily through the hallway door.*]

CECILIA   And I'll put on my hat and be right down, too.   [*She exits through the same door.*]

MANOLO   And if you feel up to it, Don José.

DON JOSÉ   Well, I'd like to...but this business with Florita...you know what fathers are like...Perhaps you could bring me a pastry and I could eat it here...And another for Florita...You don't mind, do you?

MANOLO   How could I mind! Not just one pastry! A whole dozen! And tomorrow I'm going to invite you all to eat at a restaurant in Bombilla...   [*We hear Cecilia's voice which shouts from off-stage:*]

VOICE OF CECILIA   We're ready, Manolo! Good-bye, Papa!

MANOLO   [*Answering Cecilia.*]   I'll be down right away!....Good-bye, Don José...and don't forget tomorrow...And also invite Florita... And if you want to bring anyone else, bring them...Imagine! Until my sixty reales are all gone!   [*He exits through the hallway door. Don José is left alone. He's sad and he covers his face with his hands dejectedly. The stage right door opens immediately, and Florita enters and goes to the table to the left and sits down, disconsolate.*]

FLORITA   Papa!

DON JOSÉ   Flora, my dear!   [*He goes to Florita, gives her a hug, and sits next to her.*]

FLORITA   Forgive me, Papa...Forgive me, everyone...And my aunt? And Cecilia?...

DON JOSÉ   They've just left with Manolo...He got a raise and finally they're going to get married...They've gone to buy some pastries to celebrate.

FLORITA   I'm so happy for Cecilia!

DON JOSÉ   And you, my daughter? A whole day locked in your room, without wanting anything to do with us!...

FLORITA   I'll never do it again. I'm sorry, Papa...But if you knew my suffering...And how disappointed I was when I found out I was no good at...

DON JOSÉ   No good? No good at what, dear?

FLORITA   Winking.

DON JOSÉ   Winking?

FLORITA   Yes, Papa. I've practiced for hours and hours, but I'm no good.

DON JOSÉ   Is that what you were doing in front of the mirror?

FLORITA   That's right, Papa...First I tried with one eye and then the other, but it's useless...

DON JOSÉ   And just what did you want to wink for, my dear?

FLORITA   When I spoke with Don Claudio and the priest, I assured them that if they wouldn't help me get a decent job, I would become a streetwalker.

DON JOSÉ   [*Horrified.*]   A streetwalker? You, Florita!

FLORITA   Yes, Papa. That's why I wanted to learn how to wink, so that men would follow me down the street and would say: "What a Galician!" and those things that men know how to say...

DON JOSÉ   Florita, my God!

FLORITA   But I can't...Look how badly I wink...   [*Florita closes an eye. Don José gets angry.*]

DON JOSÉ   Open that eye, you fool!

FLORITA   Yes, Papa...But I've read novels in which there are bad women who go out on the street and down to the Tabarín and there they wink for a while and right away a man invites them to dinner...

DON JOSÉ   To dinner? Those aren't novels...Those are just stories...

FLORITA   It does go on, Papa...And in those novels it says that once you know how to wink, everything else is very easy...

DON JOSÉ   Not so easy, my dear, more difficult than you think...

FLORITA   Difficult! Do you know what is really difficult? To go out on the balcony and flirt and have a student stroll after you down the street, and follow you to mass, and follow you down Recoletos, and write you a little letter, and then another, and finish his career, and speak with his parents, and his parents with your parents, and finally one day, get married!...

DON JOSÉ   Oh, I know it's not as easy as it sounds.

FLORITA   On the other hand...I have heard that five minutes after you run into a gentleman in Fornos, you are already seated at a table eating lobster and olives.

DON JOSÉ   [*Interested.*]   In just five minutes...So soon?

FLORITA   Yes, that's what they say.

DON JOSÉ   And you mean eating lobster and olives?

FLORITA   And veal au jus.

DON JOSÉ   [*His mouth watering.*]   My goodness! That's certainly not a bad menu.   [*He reacts furiously at the temptation.*]   Well, even so! Not even if there were side dishes! I will never allow you to eat such junk...

FLORITA   And I'll never do it, Papa...You know very well that I'm incapable...It's just been a foolish thought and I ask your forgiveness.   [*They hold hands emotionally and Don José, moved, speaks:*]

DON JOSÉ   You must stop fantasizing and return to reality...With the

sale of the piano, we can get by for a little while...Meanwhile, calm
down. Embroider a bit, sew on a button...Make a blouse...Go to
the kitchen and wait for the water to boil...Do what all women
do...And remember that the only road a woman has is to marry a
man...Pablo is in love with you...

FLORITA   But he hasn't asked me to marry him. He told me he would
come to see me and bring his father, and it's been four days since I've
heard from him...Besides, his salary is so low and his father is so
poor...   [*Felisa enters very happily through the hallway door.*]

FELISA   Señorita Flora! Pablo's here!

FLORITA   Pablo!

DON JOSÉ   You see? Didn't I tell you!

FELISA   With another man, older.

DON JOSÉ   His father, Florita! He's come to ask...

FLORITA   [*Nervous.*]   What do I do now? Look at my face! I've been
crying...

DON JOSÉ   Go on, Felisa, tell them to come in...

FELISA   Yes, sir.   [*She exits through the hallway door.*]

DON JOSÉ   I'll receive them while you get fixed up, and no matter what,
my dear, show your best side. Be feminine, happy, playful...Have
him see in you the woman who can bring happiness into his life for-
ever...Forget your sadness and laugh...

FLORITA   Yes, Papa...I'll laugh. Ha-ha!...

DON JOSÉ   Laugh more...Laugh like a bell...

FLORITA   Like a bell?...Ha-ha-ha!...

DON JOSÉ   Like that! Like a bell!...

FLORITA   Ha-ha-ha! Ha-ha-ha! Ha-ha-ha!   [*She exits through the stage
right door, laughing like a bell. Through the hallway door enter Pablo
and Hernández.*]

PABLO   Don José!

HERNÁNDEZ   Señor García!

DON JOSÉ   My goodness! If it isn't Señor de la Barquera!...So good to
see you!

HERNÁNDEZ   Well, here you have me; Pablo told me he was going to pay
you a visit and so I said, "I'll go with you," and here I am.   [*To
Pablo.*]   Isn't that right?

PABLO   Yes, that's how it happened.

DON JOSÉ   Well, even if it hadn't been, I'm very pleased to see you, Señor
de la Barquera...

HERNÁNDEZ   Thank you very much, Señor García.

DON JOSÉ   Sit down, sit down...   [*They all sit to the right.*]

PABLO   And Florita?

DON JOSÉ   She'll be out in a minute. I've sent word to her room but the house is so large that it will be a while before she receives the message and gets here...

HERNÁNDEZ   As long as nightfall doesn't catch her in route...

DON JOSÉ   No. I don't think she'll be that long...

HERNÁNDEZ   Well, if you knew how much I want to see Florita...I found her so pleasant. And I won't even tell you how much Pablito wants to see her. Because he loves her, Señor García. He told me so...with all his heart.

DON JOSÉ   I know, I know. And with Pablito, she's like a bell that rings.

HERNÁNDEZ   What do you mean rings? Ring, ring, ring!...

DON JOSÉ   Well, let's not argue about how many rings. What's important is that they marry and be happy. And your father, Pablito? I thought he was going to come...

PABLO   [*Sadly.*]   Yes, that's what he thought...but...he stayed home, crying.

HERNÁNDEZ   [*Also sad.*]   Yes, Señor. And my wife, too...

PABLO   And Don Claudio's wife, too.

DON JOSÉ   My goodness! Why all that mourning?

PABLO   I didn't want to tell you because I knew it would upset you, but we have been let go, Don José...

DON JOSÉ   No...

HERNÁNDEZ   Yes, sir...With the new cabinet, everything has been turned topsy-turvy. Some have been given a raise and some of us have been turned out on the street.

PABLO   Imagine our situation...

DON JOSÉ   Yes, it's serious...

PABLO   And I was thinking I could marry Florita soon!...

DON JOSÉ   And she, also.

PABLO   And now! Until I find another position...

DON JOSÉ   Don't say anything to Florita, Pablo...She thought that your visit here, this afternoon...

PABLO   That was my idea, but now...

DON JOSÉ   Don't say anything, then...

PABLO   But I wanted to explain...

DON JOSÉ   [*With sadness.*]   In any case, don't...Since they fired her from the office, her nerves haven't been good and now if she finds out about this new misfortune, she's capable of becoming a nun or poisoning herself.   [*Florita enters stage right with a new dress; she is spruced up and laughing.*]

FLORITA   Hello, Pablo, good afternoon...Oh, it's Señor Hernández! I'm so happy to see you here!...So happy! Ha-ha-ha!...

HERNÁNDEZ   I've come with Pablo, Florita.

FLORITA   What a good idea. And Don Claudio? And Ramón?

PABLO   Working, as always.

FLORITA   They're so nice! Such enjoyable people!

HERNÁNDEZ   I want you to know, Florita, that when Don Claudio fired you we all thought it an injustice and we told him so...Just like that...Right to his face...

FLORITA   I know. Pablo has already told me, and I'm very grateful. But you mustn't worry! That notion of mine about working in an office was childish, and I've not thought about it again. What a woman needs to do is forget about such foolishness—documents and gadgets—and get married, isn't that true, Pablo?...

PABLO   [*Very sad.*]   Of course.

FLORITA   Don't you think so, Señor Hernández?

HERNÁNDEZ   [*Also very sad.*]   That's right.

FLORITA   And you, Papa?

DON JOSÉ   [*Lugubrious.*]   Of course.

FLORITA   That's everything in life. A good man and a good woman. Getting married and being happy, and loving each other a lot, and laughing about everything...When some bad times come along? Well, ha-ha-ha!...If some misfortune occurs? Well, take it as a joke...Do you like happiness, Pablo?

PABLO   [*Still sad.*]   Very much.

FLORITA   And you, Señor Hernández?

HERNÁNDEZ   [*Sad also.*]   A great deal!

FLORITA   Well, if you like happiness, I'm like a bell...And I'm sure that, at my side, a man would always be happy and content. Let's laugh! Come on, let's laugh!...   [*She notices that everyone is serious.*] But what's the matter with all of you?

PABLO   Oh, nothing. We're just listening.

FLORITA   You're very serious, Papa.

DON JOSÉ   [*Trying to hide his feelings.*]   How could I be serious, standing at your side when you're a bell...I'm dying of laughter...

FLORITA   Don't lie, Papa. There's something wrong here.

PABLO   I can't hide it any more, Don José...   [*To Florita.*]   I've been let go and I can't marry you as I'd planned...

FLORITA   [*With a sigh of disappointment.*]   Let go!

HERNÁNDEZ   And so have I, Florita. And Don Claudio. And half the country...

DON JOSÉ   But he does love you and says that when this is straightened out...

FLORITA   [*With bitterness.*]   Yes, of course.   [*She rises so they don't notice her emotion.*]   It's all right, don't worry...It's just that I was so happy and then suddenly this...Poor Pablo! Poor Señor Hernández!...Men's lives are also affected!

DON JOSÉ   You don't realize how much, Florita...

FLORITA   All right, Papa, don't worry...It will all get straightened out...   [*Doña Matilde and Cecilia enter excitedly through the hallway door; they sit down, exhausted and disconsolate, in some chairs.*]

DOÑA MATILDE   Good afternoon. Hello, Don Justo Hernández de la Barquera.

HERNÁNDEZ   Good afternoon, Señora...

PABLO   Good afternoon, Doña Matilde.

CECILIA   My heavens, what a bad time we had!

DON JOSÉ   But, what's wrong?

FLORITA   What's happened, Aunt?

DON JOSÉ   Did you lose my pastries?

DOÑA MATILDE   For heaven's sake, don't talk to me about pastries...

DON JOSÉ   Then tell us what's wrong...

DOÑA MATILDE   [*Between sobs.*]   We went to the pastry shop where Manolo had invited us...

CECILIA   [*Also sobbing.*]   And there we were, just as happy as...

DOÑA MATILDE   Until Manolo ran into a friend who was coming from the Ministry. He told him that they had just agreed to cancel the fifteen peseta raise to all functionaries because it would mean the ruin of the country and that panic had set in throughout the nation...

CECILIA   Just imagine! Manolo got pale.

DOÑA MATILDE   And although he insisted that we go ahead, he had such a horrible look on his face that we said good-bye and came running home while Manolo went back to the Ministry to return the fifteen pesetas...

DON JOSÉ   Isn't this just great!

DOÑA MATILDE   And of course, Manolo can no longer marry Cecilia...

CECILIA   [*She rises, her nerves at the breaking point.*]   I'm desperate and I want to die! Why so much sacrifice and so much hat and so much balcony? How long is this constant turmoil going to last,...and the insomnia, and these frayed nerves? Because this is no longer a struggle between a woman and a man, but a crisis...with the government, with the whole world!...And I can't stand it any more. I'm going to have an attack, but before I do, I want to go to my room and cry...   [*She exits crying through the hallway.*]

HERNÁNDEZ   Who was that young woman?

FLORITA   She's my sister, Señor Hernández.

HERNÁNDEZ   Oh, I see! Well, she's very pretty!

DOÑA MATILDE   And she was so happy, thinking she was going to marry Manolo...But at least, Florita, there's you and Pablo...

PABLO   I've been let go, Señora.

DOÑA MATILDE   What did you say?

HERNÁNDEZ   We've both been let go. . .

DOÑA MATILDE   Is this possible?

FLORITA   Yes, Aunt. . . Anything is possible now. . .

DOÑA MATILDE   And now. . .

FLORITA   [*She rises slowly, piously resigned.*]   And now, nothing. . .
Everything will stay the same. . . I tried to rebel against destiny, to
move ahead of our times and our customs, and I failed. . . Now I'm
deeply sorry, because in life we have to be humble and simple and
follow the path that the Lord has chosen for us with faith and Chris-
tian resignation. . . And confronted with the idea of being publicly
alone, I prefer another kind of solitude. . . the saintly solitude of the
cloister. . .   [*And she stands quietly, looking down.*]

DOÑA MATILDE   Heavens!

DON JOSÉ   It's cloroanemia, Señor Hernández.

HERNÁNDEZ   But in its acutest stage. I know about these things!   [*The
curtains close. Again we hear the background music; Felisa appears stage
left and, over the music, explains to the public:*]

FELISA   Señorita Flora, naturally, did not become a nun, because she had
no vocation. And four or five days later she recovered from her crisis
and took up the usual life of a young lady of her time: that is, she
waited patiently for Pablo to find a job while she embroidered a
flower on a little piece of cloth. And I, who years later was employed
in the post office and sold stamps at the communications building – I
was one of the nicer ones who always stuck the stamps on the letters
and had the correct change – have never forgotten her, because
Señorita Flora was a precursor and a prophet, and she initiated some
customs in our house that turned the whole neighborhood upside
down. . . For example, I, like most all the maids of that time, was
only allowed to go out for a stroll one out of ten Sundays, and then
only from 4:15 until 4:50. And if I returned a little late, well, I had to
face a council of war and they locked me in the pantry for two or
three days. . . Well, Señorita Flora, with those very original ideas of
hers, was able to get them to let me go out every third Sunday. And
instead of having to return at 4:50, with my tongue hanging out, I
could return at 5:15, which was a great relief, especially for my boyfriend, who never had time for all those things that boyfriends want
to do. That's why I've never forgotten Señorita Flora and I fre-
quently remember what happened on the day that everything
changed for us, the poor, unprotected women. . .   [*The curtains
have opened with the last words of Felisa and we see Florita, who is
embroidering. When Felisa exits right, Manolo enters through the hallway door.*]

MANOLO   News, Florita! I've got news!

FLORITA [*Without paying much attention.*] Good or the usual?

MANOLO Fantastic! I've seen Don Claudio and it seems that the new minister of his branch is a good friend of his; and besides being a friend, he's a big smoker, one of those who smokes only those cigarettes with the special tips...And since Don Claudio is a demon at rolling special tipped cigarettes, he's been appointed Director General...

FLORITA How wonderful! What else?

MANOLO Don Claudio told the Minister about the experiment he tried with you and how useful you were and how nicely you spoke through the little window and how quickly you worked with that gadget. And they've decided to create a new office in which only young women will work and where you will be the boss...And Don Claudio is going to come to tell you personally, because he wants you to be in charge of finding young women to work there...And you'll have a good salary...Which makes you happy, right?

FLORITA [*Without any illusion.*] And what friends does Don Claudio want me to find? Do other women exist who want to find a job and work? You know what I did was a failure...My friends neither speak to me nor greet me. No, Manolo, it's best to just let me embroider...

MANOLO But embroidering is dumb!

FLORITA I know...But what can I do?

MANOLO [*Disconcerted.*] Well, I brought the message and in truth, I can't understand...Anyway...Good-bye, Florita... [*When he exits upstage, he almost runs into Valentina, who enters.*]

MANOLO Excuse me, Valentina...

VALENTINA Good-bye, Manolo... [*Manolo exits and Valentina approaches Flora with a friendly and guarded expression.*] Florita...

FLORITA Oh, it's you! What do you want, Valentina?

VALENTINA I came to see you...But as I was about to enter, I heard Manolo speaking and I listened in the hallway...

FLORITA Oh, very well! And what did you want?

VALENTINA I want you to forgive me...

FLORITA Forgive you? For what?

VALENTINA My sarcasm, my unkindness. And the fact that I stopped greeting you...Because I now realize that you were right...We're in a bad way at home. Papa will never again be able to work...my boyfriend has left me, and I don't have the strength to find another...

FLORITA It's very hard, Valentina...

VALENTINA I know, Florita...And now that I've heard what Manolo said, I would like you to recommend me to work in that office...

FLORITA   [*She gets up happily.*]   Would you?...

VALENTINA   If you'll forgive me...

FLORITA   Of course, Valentina! How could I not! We'll both go to work in
an office and that way there will be two of us and we'll be stronger to
fight against those who criticize us now..., and who will criticize us
later without ever realizing why young women went to work...
[*She goes to the typewriter and takes off its cover.*]   Come here; give
me those sheets of paper!...I have to write down your name and
address to take to the Director General. What's your full name?

VALENTINA   Valentina Rodríguez Guzmán.

FLORITA   Where were you born?

VALENTINA   In Madrid.

FLORITA   How old are you?

VALENTINA   [*Lying.*]   Seventeen.

FLORITA   [*Also lying.*]   Oh, yes, three years younger than I.   [*Cecilia
appears through the hallway door and approaches the table where
Florita is writing.*]

CECILIA   Flora...

FLORITA   Hello, Cecilia.

CECILIA   Manolo just told me about Don Claudio...And he told me that
since they're not going to raise his salary, maybe I could work in your
office. And then, since we would both be earning...

FLORITA   [*Distracted.*]   Your name?

CECILIA   I'm your sister, Florita!...

FLORITA   Ah, that's true.   [*She continues writing. Doña Matilde and
Felisa enter through the hallway door and approach Florita.*]

DOÑA MATILDE   Florita, I thought if age doesn't matter, perhaps the
cash register job...

FLORITA   Your name, please?

DOÑA MATILDE   Matilde García Segura...

FLORITA   Very well. Next...

FELISA   Señorita...If only to paste the stamps...If you could find a
place for me there...I paste stamps very well...   [*Manolo enters
through the hallway, followed by Don José and Pablo. From a distance
they observe the five women.*]

MANOLO   Do you see?

DON JOSÉ   Daughter of mine!

PABLO   Florita!...

FLORITA   Just a moment, Pablo...   [*To the women.*]   Go on...It
would be best if you would each take a piece of paper and start putting down the information with a pencil...Sit here at this table...

DOÑA MATILDE   Yes, dear, yes...

FELISA   Yes, Señorita...   [*Florita takes Pablo to the right while Doña*

Matilde, Cecilia, Valentina, and Felisa sit down on four chairs at the table and begin to write.]

FLORITA   Pablo, I'm very grateful to you for the interest you've always shown in me, but I believe that...for the moment...we shouldn't think about that. Perhaps in the future...

PABLO   But why, Florita?

DON JOSÉ   Why daughter?

FLORITA   Because now I must concentrate on my work and my employees...if you just knew what hopes I have for our office of young women! I want it to be a place where more work is done, and with more attention, and where there are no arguments and no one speaks louder than anyone else, where everyone works in silence, just as they are working now!...   [*At that moment, and in very screechy tones they begin to speak, two by two, with crossing conversations, as they did in the first act: Matilde with Cecilia and Valentina with Felisa.*]

DOÑA MATILDE   [*To Cecilia.*]   Your birthdate should be above the address.

CECILIA   No, Aunt, I think it's just the opposite...

DOÑA MATILDE   But how could it be the opposite, Cecilia!

CECILIA   That's how Florita wrote it before...

DOÑA MATILDE   Well, if that's the way she wrote it, she must be right because I've never seen a more intelligent young woman...

CECILIA   I'm very happy because this way, I won't have to be at home all day with Manolo.

DOÑA MATILDE   Naturally. Being at home all day gets very boring.

CECILIA   Manolo can come by for me every day when I get off...

DOÑA MATILDE   Since his ministry is near ours, he can do it on the way.

VALENTINA   [*To Florita.*]   I can't wait to go home and give Mother the news...

FELISA   Maybe your family won't take it too well...

VALENTINA   Actually, the problem was that they were jealous of Florita...

FELISA   Well, of course, but now, when I go out every Sunday, they'll also be jealous of me...

VALENTINA   But don't you go out every Sunday now?

FELISA   No, Señorita...every nine Sundays only, and I go out at 4:00 and I have to be back at 5:00.

VALENTINA   In my house, up till now, we've let them return at 5:30, but they couldn't go out until 5:00...

FELISA   Each home has its own customs...

VALENTINA   Little by little, these customs will be disappearing...

FELISA   Yes, yes...but until the customs disappear...   [*As this pair begins the conversation, Florita has separated herself from Pablo and has joined the group of women and has begun to speak at the same time so that the noise is louder and not a word of what they're saying can be understood.*]

FLORITA   Excuse me a minute, Pablo.   [*To the women.*]   I think while you are writing down your names, I can type a report on each of you and that way I can give my opinion about the position you ought to occupy...because based on the report that I prepare and the position we each have...   [*Pablo, Don José, and Manolo have taken a seat on the sofa and watch them. The noise increases. The curtain falls slowly.*]

THE END

The Enchanting Dorotea

The Enchanting Dorotea

A Comedy in Two Acts

Characters (in order of appearance)

BENITA

INÉS

REMEDIOS

DON MANUEL

DOÑA RITA

ROSA

DOROTEA

JUAN

JOSÉ

The play takes place in a small
seaside town in northern Spain;
it is any year before World War I.

ACT ONE

Scene 1

A small sitting room in the home of Dorotea; it has a comfortable, but provincial, atmosphere. Downstage right is a door that is closed. Next to the door, and set at an angle, is a balcony with shutters and curtains. In the upstage wall is a door that opens to a hallway. There is another door to the left. Downstage right is a large chest of drawers; next to it, a rocking chair. To the right, a large lamptable surrounded by three chairs. There is other furniture appropriate for the room: pictures, lithographs, and paintings on the walls. It is dark, just before dawn, and the lamps are lighted. As the curtain opens, Benita, Inés, and Remedios are seated in the room. They are young women of the town and wear black, with veils. Inés and Remedios also carry umbrellas. They are listening to the sound of a heavy rainstorm.

BENITA   I think the weather is settling down.

INÉS   It looks like it.

BENITA   I really think it's going to clear up.

REMEDIOS   That would certainly suit me!

INÉS   Maybe the sun will even come out.   [*She rises and goes toward the balcony to look, lifting the curtain.*]

REMEDIOS   I doubt it—where would it come out *to* on a day like this?

INÉS   At any rate, we always have at least one good afternoon in August.

BENITA   That's because it's the best month. . .think what it's like in July! Good Heavens!

REMEDIOS   It was extremely unpleasant yesterday.

INÉS   The north wind was the most unpleasant part.

REMEDIOS   Why, our summer resident was almost drowned.

BENITA   But, we still have one left, don't we?

INÉS   Heavens, no! He went back to Madrid the day before yesterday. . .with a cold, he said. It was the day of the hailstorm.   [*Sits down again next to her friends.*]

BENITA   That was an *extremely* unpleasant hailstorm.

REMEDIOS   It even spooked my father's mule.

INÉS   The black one?

REMEDIOS   No, the grey.

BENITA   Well, that one always gets spooked.

INÉS   Yes, it's always been like that.

REMEDIOS   The veterinarian says what's wrong is that the mule has an inferiority. . .something or other.

INÉS   I wouldn't be a bit surprised.

REMEDIOS   You know how it is with mules; there's always something. [*The door to the right opens and Don Manuel enters. He is in his sixties and wears black pants with suspenders outside his shirt. He passes in front of the women, who rise, and he goes toward the chest of drawers.*]

DON MANUEL   Morning.

THE THREE WOMEN   Good morning. [*Don Manuel opens a drawer and looks through it, searching for something that he does not find.*]

BENITA   You must be nervous, right? [*Don Manuel, as an answer, emits a meaningless grunt.*]

INÉS   On a day like this you're supposed to be nervous, Don Manuel... say you are!

REMEDIOS   My father, the poor thing, is always nervous.

BENITA   And he's never been in *this* situation, Reme. [*Don Manuel, after looking through everything, turns and exits right, closing the door after bidding good-bye to the young women.*]

DON MANUEL   Good-bye.

THE THREE WOMEN   Good-bye. [*After Don Manuel exits, the three sit down again, and speak in a low voice.*]

BENITA   Did you notice?

INÉS   I knew it.

REMEDIOS   He's a nervous wreck.

BENITA   Well, it doesn't surprise me.

INÉS   In these circumstances. [*Loud thunder.*]

REMEDIOS   Sounds like it's getting worse.

BENITA   Perhaps a tiny bit. [*She gets up and looks through the balcony curtains.*]

REMEDIOS   Well, if we're having bad weather here, just think what it must be like in Madrid.

INÉS   I don't even want to imagine it.

BENITA   I don't know how they can live in such a place.

REMEDIOS   They're suicidal, Beni.

INÉS   Of course, and...

BENITA   And then they arrive here and complain that there's a water shortage.

INÉS   If they hadn't wasted it all in Madrid...

REMEDIOS   And on vices, besides.

BENITA   And what vices. Did I tell you that the summer resident, the one with the cold, asked me one day if we didn't have a greased pole? [*She sits down again next to her friends.*]

REMEDIOS   Imagine! As if we would have such indecent things here!

INÉS   People come here for the sun and nothing else.

BENITA   And for our famous procession.   [*Doña Rita enters right. She is Dorotea's aunt and is about 45 years old; she is dressed in robe and slippers. She also goes to the chest of drawers, where she looks for something.*]

DOÑA RITA   Good morning.

THE THREE WOMEN   [*Rising.*]   Good morning.

REMEDIOS   You must be very nervous?   [*Rita doesn't answer.*]

INÉS   You're supposed to be nervous today.

BENITA   In these circumstances.

REMEDIOS   And when you're on edge...

INÉS   It's hard to control yourself...

REMEDIOS   I always say that nerves are a real problem, don't you think so, Doña Rita?   [*Rita doesn't find what she's looking for in the chest of drawers and exits right, saying good-bye as she leaves.*]

DOÑA RITA   Good-bye.

THE THREE WOMEN   Good-bye.   [*They return to their seats and begin whispering again.*]

INÉS   She's the worst one in the family. Dorotea's father is repulsive, but at least he has money. And once was a councilman! But his sister! She's been living off him ever since her husband died.

REMEDIOS   And what airs she puts on!

BENITA   She treated us like dirt!

REMEDIOS   I think maybe they're just upset because we're here so early.   [*In the distance, a church bell is heard.*]

INÉS   Early? Six-fifteen in the morning?

BENITA   The sun is coming up!...   [*Rosa, the maid, enters from the left. She is plain, a little coarse. She also looks for something in the chest of drawers.*]

ROSA   Hello.

BENITA   Hello, Rosa.

ROSA   Are you still waiting?

INÉS   Obviously. Since we haven't seen Dorotea yet.

ROSA   You haven't seen her? That's odd.

REMEDIOS   How can she take so long getting dressed?

ROSA   Maybe she isn't getting ready. Maybe she's still in bed...you know how she is.

BENITA   [*Irritated.*]   Are you going to tell us that she's not awake yet?

INÉS   [*Also irritated.*]   You must be joking!

ROSA   I haven't seen her at all this morning.

REMEDIOS   Well, go see where she is.

INÉS   And tell her we're here.

ROSA   [*Closing the drawer.*]   All right. I'll go see...   [*She starts toward the upstage door, but Benita stops her.*]

BENITA   Wait! I'll bet you're nervous, right?

ROSA   Me?

REMEDIOS   If you really care about Dorotea, you must be.

INÉS   And she must be...

ROSA   [*Coldly.*]   If you say so.   [*She leaves calmly through the upstage door.*]

INÉS   Can you believe it?

BENITA   No one can get anything out of her.

REMEDIOS   This whole family is strange, even the maid.

INÉS   And what are they all looking for in the chest of drawers?

REMEDIOS   I don't know. Maybe they have mice...   [*Rosa's voice is heard, as well as knocking on a door.*]

ROSA   [*Offstage.*]   Señorita Dorotea? Señorita Dorotea?

REMEDIOS   Do you hear?

BENITA   Yes.

INÉS   She's probably fainted...

BENITA   I wouldn't be surprised.

ROSA   [*Offstage.*]   Señorita Dorotea!

REMEDIOS   [*Getting up.*]   I'm going to see what's happening...

INÉS   No, Reme! Be still! Wait...

REMEDIOS   I can't stand it...

BENITA   You must...

REMEDIOS   [*Goes toward the upstage door.*]   Here she comes again.   [*Rosa enters, smiling.*]

ROSA   Didn't I tell you?

INÉS   What?

REMEDIOS   What happened?

ROSA   The Señorita was sound asleep. I know it's hard to believe...but she was sound asleep.

REMEDIOS   [*Outraged.*]   Don't tell me she was sleeping!

INÉS   [*Also angry.*]   That can't be!

ROSA   Didn't you hear how loud I had to knock to wake her? She was really asleep...like a log...dead to the world...

BENITA   That's probably because she couldn't sleep all night!

ROSA   Oh, no. She went to bed at eight; she started reading one of those French novels she likes and when I took her a glass of milk at nine, she was out like a light. That means she's slept for ten hours straight!

REMEDIOS   [*Indignant.*]   That's a lie, Rosa!

INÉS   You are not telling the truth!

REMEDIOS   Can't you see, they're playing games with us.   [*She goes back and sits down in her original seat.*]

ROSA   Games? What games?   [*Moving toward the door at the rear.*]

Look, here she comes... still half asleep.

[*Dorotea enters. About twenty-five or thirty years old. Also a smalltown woman, but different; she is more sophisticated than the other three women and has an amused air of superiority.*]

DOROTEA   Good morning, girls... I'm so sorry...

THE THREE WOMEN   Good morning, Dorotea.

DOROTEA   Rosa told me you were here... is something the matter? Why so early?   [*While Dorotea is speaking, Rosa pulls back the balcony curtains and lets in the morning sun.*]

BENITA   It's already past six, Dorotea.

DOROTEA   I know. But, why are you looking at me like that?

REMEDIOS   Rosa told us you were asleep.

DOROTEA   [*Sitting in the rocking chair.*]   Yes, I was. It was marvelous... I was sleeping so well!

INÉS   [*Indignant.*]   That can't be true! Don't lie to us, Dorotea.

DOROTEA   Why can't it be true?

REMEDIOS   How could you be sleeping... when you're getting married today in just two hours?

DOROTEA   Oh, that's right! It *is* today! I'd forgotten! You know how I am about these things... are you sure it's today?

ROSA   Of course it is, Señorita. I reminded you yesterday at noon...

DOROTEA   Oh, yes! How could I have forgotten... I even wrote it down somewhere...   [*She gets up and addresses Rosa.*]   Well, Rosa, go get the veil and things ready... although now that I think about it, I'm not sure we bought a veil...

ROSA   I saw something white in your bedroom yesterday... white and long...

DOROTEA   That's probably it. You'd better go iron it, Rosa... it must be terribly wrinkled.

ROSA   Yes, Señorita. I'll go right away.   [*Exits upstage.*]

DOROTEA   How could I have overslept! What a disgrace! And on such a special day! Now I'll be late!

BENITA   That's enough, Dorotea!

INÉS   Yes... we've had enough!

DOROTEA   Enough of what?

REMEDIOS   Enough of your joking.

DOROTEA   I don't understand.

BENITA   I won't tolerate your making fun of us!

INÉS   You weren't sleeping!

REMEDIOS   When a woman like you is finally getting married, she doesn't sleep, she doesn't eat... she doesn't even breathe...

DOROTEA   Has this been your personal experience?

REMEDIOS   At least when my time comes, I won't try to conceal my feelings as you're doing in order to make myself important. You want to humiliate us or drive us crazy—just so you can be original...

INÉS   I never thought you'd do this to your best friends, Dorotea!

BENITA   This is too much!

DOROTEA   I don't understand what you're so excited about.

REMEDIOS   When the whole town has been unable to sleep, thinking about your wedding, how could you have been asleep?

DOROTEA   It all depends on how badly one wants to get married...

INÉS   You don't want to?

DOROTEA   Like everyone else, when I was nineteen I wanted to. But now, at twenty-five, the whole thing seems such a bother. Imagine having a man sleep in the same bed with you! How awful!

BENITA   Everything you're saying is a lie.

INÉS   You don't mean it!

REMEDIOS   You're just trying to make us mad.

DOROTEA   Why did you come here today? Just to start a fight?   [*She pulls up a chair next to her friends.*]

BENITA   We came to see what you were doing, to find out how nervous you were. So we could tell the rest of the town.

DOROTEA   But why would I be nervous? I don't understand...

REMEDIOS   Because you're finally getting married. Isn't that enough?

DOROTEA   And who am I marrying, may I ask? Some good-for-nothing from Madrid who's only after my money.

REMEDIOS   [*Her irritation disappears. All three regain their calm.*] Well, yes, that's true...

BENITA   We have to agree with you on that...

INÉS   We can't deny the obvious...

DOROTEA   A fortune hunter who wants to marry me in order to end up with a hotel and restaurant, five meat markets, a wine shop, twenty houses, and fifty cows, all of which I will inherit when my father dies.

INÉS   Of course.

DOROTEA   Isn't that what they're saying in town?

BENITA   Something like that...why should we lie to you?

DOROTEA   And isn't that what you think, too?

REMEDIOS   Not exactly...but he *is* a nobody.

INÉS   And you have to remember that you've rejected the best young men in town.

BENITA   Because they weren't good enough for you.

REMEDIOS   Including my brother Dionisio.

DOROTEA   Your brother Dionisio is an idiot.

REMEDIOS   How dare you insult my brother!

DOROTEA   An idiot, who on the first day we went out, asked me: Aside from the properties and the restaurant and the cattle, how much actual cold, hard cash will you inherit when your father dies – which is bound to be soon?

REMEDIOS   That's because Dionisio wants to expand his store and needs money.

INÉS   We all told you he would be right for you. And it's true. He's a very good person.

BENITA   The truth is we're the only friends you have. No one else can stand you.

REMEDIOS   And not because you're rich... but because you're strange.

INÉS   Just because you spent eight days in Bayonne, you think you're better than anybody else.

DOROTEA   It wasn't eight. It was ten. And I have the receipts to prove it in the chest of drawers.   [*She goes toward the chest of drawers.*]

BENITA   But you spent six days on the train.

DOROTEA   Only three days on the train...

REMEDIOS   Anyway, what does Bayonne have that we don't have here?

DOROTEA   They're freer there. They aren't preoccupied with the lives of others. They live, breathe, kiss, love. They do what they want to.

BENITA   You've always done what you want. You've always been a spoiled darling. A brat.

DOROTEA   Because I'm a rebel. Because the things you take seriously, I don't. Because this disagreeable conversation, which you are engaging in, makes me smile instead of irritating me. And because I don't give a damn what the town thinks.

INÉS   That's not true. You're afraid of the town, just like the rest of us. You're afraid of what they'll say, of the gossip...

BENITA   And you protect yourself with defiance and scorn.

REMEDIOS   And that is dangerous, Dorotea. Because the town has power.

DOROTEA   But power to do what? To say, as they are saying now, as they have said of all those before him, that Fermín doesn't love me and is only marrying me for my money? To smile knowingly when we walk down Main Street? What would make them happy? To be rich is a crime. To be poor is worse. They laugh if you do *not* marry; if you do, they laugh more. If the summer people do not come from Madrid to this town that offers only storms, sardines, and, as a major attraction, fireworks – if they don't come, the town claims they're cretins. If they do come, and a young woman crosses her legs or orders a drink in a cafe, she's a tramp. The townspeople are against everything. And I'm against them.

REMEDIOS   But you're making enemies for nothing.

DOROTEA   Everyone here is an enemy. For example...   [*She returns and sits down.*]   why haven't I married before? And why haven't you? Because as soon as we showed any interest in someone, the town found something wrong with him. This one drank. That one didn't go to mass. Another had a lover in Barcelona. One of them had epilepsy as a child. They didn't say these things to protect us but to destroy us. Yet with these comments ringing in our ears, we would end the relationship and wander again down Main Street hoping to find someone who would satisfy them.

BENITA   You may be right.

DOROTEA   And in this search, who did we find? Only men who wanted to take advantage of us. And for the last four months, not even that. You know what's happened since the Mayor ordered streetlights for the park; all the young men have stopped seeing us and have started playing football instead. Because what they wanted was the darkness, the anonymity, and the deceit. That's all they cared about. Is that true or not?

INÉS   It's true.

REMEDIOS   The matter is so serious that the City Council is going to debate it. They're going to decide whether to turn out the lights altogether or to have them on only every other day.

DOROTEA   So, if you've come here to see how I am, go home and say that I'm very nervous, that I didn't sleep at all, that I'm having palpitations and that they'll probably have to carry me to the church on a stretcher. Will that make you happy?   [*She returns the chair to its former position.*]

BENITA   I hope we haven't said anything to make you mad.

INÉS   We came as your friends.

REMEDIOS   And you must admit that you're the one who's being difficult.

DOROTEA   I know. I'm sorry. But I just woke up and I'm still so sleepy...   [*She sits down in the rocking chair.*]

REMEDIOS   [*Furious.*]   Not that again!   [*She goes toward her.*]

BENITA   [*Angry also.*]   You can't be serious!

INÉS   [*Equally mad.*]   Why do you keep saying that?
   [*Don Manuel enters from the right. He is dressed in black for the wedding, with a Derby, cane, and gloves.*]

DON MANUEL   Good morning.

DOROTEA   [*Goes to him and kisses him.*]   Good morning, Papa.

DON MANUEL   I'm all ready, Dorotea. Why aren't you getting dressed?

DOROTEA   It's still early. Anyway, I was just saying good-bye to my friends.

DON MANUEL   Well, do it then. It's time they left for home.

BENITA   We were just leaving.

DON MANUEL   I certainly hope so!   [*He sits down in a chair, downstage, next to the right entrance.*]

INÉS   We *must* go so they can help you dress.

DOROTEA   All I have to do is slip on a dress and put that white thing on my head.

BENITA   We have to get ready too, because we want to be the first ones at the church so we won't miss anything.

DOROTEA   Well, hurry then, so you won't be late.

BENITA   We'll give you our best wishes now.   [*The three kiss her.*]

REMEDIOS   Don't be too nervous...

DOROTEA   Do I look nervous?

INÉS   We never thought you'd be so calm...

BENITA   Good-bye, Don Manuel.

DON MANUEL   Go to the devil.

REMEDIOS   We'll see you shortly.

DOROTEA   Good-bye, good-bye.   [*The three friends exit right. As soon as they've gone, Dorotea closes the door, and begins to panic. She runs back and forth as if looking for something, and then goes to the chest of drawers and begins to search through the drawers as have the other members of the household.*]

DOROTEA   I'm so nervous! I'm going to be late! What have I done with my makeup?

DON MANUEL   What did those magpies have to say?

DOROTEA   Nothing. The same old thing.

DON MANUEL   Why were they screeching?

DOROTEA   Because I told them I'd been sleeping until a few minutes ago, and they couldn't stand it.

DON MANUEL   It's not true, is it?

DOROTEA   I didn't sleep all night, Papa. I've been up since 4 o'clock, taking a bath, roaming the hall.

DON MANUEL   It's a wonder we didn't run into each other because I was doing the same thing.

DOROTEA   That's because I stayed in my lane.

DON MANUEL   And I stayed in mine.

DOROTEA   I *did* run into Rosa, who was also pacing the floor, and that's when we made up the story about my having slept all night. My God, I'm so nervous!

DON MANUEL   [*Rises and goes toward Dorotea.*]   What a rotten life this is, Dorotea! All of us making each other miserable!

DOROTEA   We have to defend ourselves, Papa. Otherwise, they'll devour us...

DON MANUEL   While I was getting dressed, I heard you say that Fermín was marrying you only for your money. Is that really what you think?

DOROTEA   That's what they think and what the whole town thinks. And

I wanted to say it to them before they said it to me. But Fermín and I love each other. Fermín is the only noble and decent person I've known since I was a girl. And we want to marry each other, which we will do—and we will be very happy, if I can only find that makeup case...

DON MANUEL   What do you need the makeup case for, damn it!   [*He goes back and sits down at the table.*]

DOROTEA   I *don't* really need it...I'm just so nervous...Oh, my God, I'm going to be late for the ceremony!   [*Rosa enters upstage, dressed for the wedding and also very nervous.*]

ROSA   Come on, Señorita, I have everything ready. You have to hurry!

DOROTEA   I know, Rosa...I'm coming.   [*She starts to exit right.*]

ROSA   Not that way...your room is this way...

DOROTEA   Oh, that's right! I'm so confused! Where do I go?

ROSA   This way...down the hall...I'll lead the way...just follow me...   [*Rosa exits upstage.*]

DOROTEA   I'm right behind you. I'll be back, Papa. Don't get undressed, all right? Don't change your clothes...

[*Dorotea exits, following Rosa. Rita enters right, also dressed for the wedding.*]

RITA   Where's Dorotea?

DON MANUEL   She's getting dressed.

RITA   I'll go help her.

DON MANUEL   No, stay here. Rosa's helping her.

RITA   Why was she arguing with her friends?

DON MANUEL   You know how she can be...no one can tolerate her.

RITA   How well I know! At least she is finally getting married! Maybe she'll stop being so odd.

DON MANUEL   Well, she is unusual.

RITA   Just like her mother, may she rest in peace. Totally extravagant! Anyone would know she was from Orihuela!...

DON MANUEL   Don't bring up her mother or you'll be sorry.   [*Raises his cane.*]

RITA   I've heard you say the same thing yourself.

DON MANUEL   I can say whatever I want because of who I am. But you're only my sister, and you can't. Anyway, if she's odd, she has her reasons.

RITA   I don't know what they are.

DON MANUEL   She's been jilted many times, Rita. And with no explanation. I've often wondered...

RITA   It's because of the way she is!

DON MANUEL   I'm not so sure.

RITA   What else could it be?

DON MANUEL   I don't know . . . whatever it was, I never understood it. Sometimes, of course, *she* rejected them. But the result has been the same.

RITA   She's too proud.

DON MANUEL   She's too intelligent. It's only natural that she doesn't get along with these local fools, who are full of hypocrisy, as are you and I. Especially you.

RITA   She's as much a fool as we are, even though she doesn't think so.

DON MANUEL   She has her own ideas. She knows French. She's traveled. And she has a sense of her own independence. She's a rebel.

RITA   There's no room for rebellion in this town. We all have to be like everyone else.

DON MANUEL   The town is changing, Rita. It's different. We have the summer tourists, now.

RITA   We've had two this year, and one has already left. If the weather doesn't change, we won't even have one . . .

DON MANUEL   But as soon as we raise the prices, more will come. That's what Dorotea thinks, and so does Fermín . . . who's a clever man. Raise the prices . . . it's a matter of cost. If we make things expensive enough, the place will be swarming with people.

RITA   Are you really going to put them in charge of the restaurant and hotel?

DON MANUEL   Of course. I've told you all about the new ideas they have. No more of these six-course dinners, which are quite ordinary . . . instead, one course . . . but with lettuce. And more expensive than six.

RITA   But what am *I* going to do then?

DON MANUEL   You'll take care of this house. And of me. And straighten out that chest of drawers so we can *find* things in it.

RITA   And the meat markets?

DON MANUEL   I'll take care of them myself.

RITA   And the cattle?

DON MANUEL   Leave that to me.

RITA   I knew that as soon as Dorotea got married, you'd take away all my responsibilities.

DON MANUEL   Because you don't know anything about business.

RITA   But Andrés helps me.

DON MANUEL   He knows even less than you.

RITA   And when you're gone, do you think Dorotea and her husband will be able to manage? You know how she is. She's a romantic. She's always been that way, she can't be bothered . . . and he . . .

[*Rosa enters from upstage and goes toward the left exit.*]

DON MANUEL   Where are you going?

ROSA   There's someone at the door.   [*Exits.*]

RITA   Another visitor . . .   [*She moves upstage.*]   I'm going to see Dorotea.

DON MANUEL   Wait a minute. What were you going to say about him?

RITA   That he would like to live in Madrid.

DON MANUEL   He has a job there and he's a decent man who doesn't
want to take advantage . . . or live off of us. But I wouldn't allow it.
Because if he marries Dorotea — and I did give permission for that —
he must take care of my affairs here, since they are also her affairs.
This was the condition I set.

RITA   You didn't need to do that. I've always helped you, and I could
have remained in charge.

DON MANUEL   But isn't it better for you to devote yourself to taking care
of me? I'm not well. I'm old. And with Dorotea going to live above
the restaurant, I'll be lonely. I'll miss her . . . in spite of her whims . . .
[*Rosa enters left, with a sealed letter in her hand. She is stunned and is
crying.*]

ROSA   This letter just arrived for Señorita Dorotea. It's from Señor
Fermín.

DON MANUEL   From Fermín?

ROSA   A boy from the boarding house brought it.   [*She begins to sob.*]

RITA   What's the matter with you?

ROSA   The boy said that Señor Fermín has gone.

DON MANUEL   What did you say?

ROSA   That he left on the first bus this morning.

DON MANUEL   That's not possible! Give me that letter!

ROSA   Here it is.

RITA   What could have happened?

DON MANUEL   I don't know if I should open this, Rita . . .

RITA   Yes, open it.

DON MANUEL   I hate to . . .
[*Dorotea enters upstage, dressed as a bride. She is happy and smiling.*]

DOROTEA   Well, what do you think? Will I do? Is this length all right, or
should I shorten it a little more?   [*She sees that everyone is
silent.*]   What's wrong?

DON MANUEL   Fermín has sent you this letter.

DOROTEA   A letter? Give it to me. Have you read it?

DON MANUEL   No.

DOROTEA   What could be wrong?   [*She opens the letter and reads it. Her
expression gradually becomes sadder.*]

RITA   What does it say?

DON MANUEL   Say something. Read it out loud.

ROSA   What's wrong, Señorita?

DOROTEA   He says that he can't marry me. That he's going back to Madrid.

DON MANUEL   But why?

DOROTEA   [*Staring at the letter.*]   He says that he thought about it all night. That everybody in town says that he's marrying me for my money...that people are laughing at him...that yesterday, in the cafe, he overheard some comments that embarrassed him. That he's become more uncomfortable and feels more ridiculous every day, and that...   [*She reads aloud from the letter.*]   "...I've made up my mind and nothing will persuade me to change it. By the time you read this, I will be far away. It would be impossible for me to live in a town where people were constantly talking about the two of us..." And other things. And asks me to forgive him. And good-bye. [*She stops looking at the letter.*]   That I forgive. How thoughtful.

DON MANUEL   How cruel, you mean!

RITA   It's incredible!

DOROTEA   Who brought the letter, Rosa?

ROSA   The boy from the boarding house. He told me Senor Fermín left an hour ago...

DOROTEA   He was amused, wasn't he?

ROSA   I told him off, Señorita...he was almost laughing...

DON MANUEL   The man is despicable!

DOROTEA   Then so are the townspeople.

DON MANUEL   I'll find him and bring him back!

DOROTEA   It would be useless...he's made up his mind...I've been jilted, and that's that.   [*She sits down next to the table.*]

DON MANUEL   Why aren't you crying? Why aren't you angry? Say something!

DOROTEA   What do you want me to say? There's nothing anyone can do. There's no reason to worry about it. If I don't marry him, I'll marry someone else.

RITA   Someone else?

DON MANUEL   Who?

DOROTEA   Anyone. It's just a matter of walking down Main Street again. I still have admirers. For example, Reme's brother, Dionisio, who wants to expand his business. Or the telegraph operator, the short one...

RITA   This is not the time for this sort of thing, Dorotea...

DOROTEA   I think it's the perfect time. I'm dressed as a bride, and the priest and the guests are waiting in the church.

DON MANUEL   What are you trying to say?

DOROTEA [*Rises and speaks firmly.*]   That I've put on my wedding
dress to get married and that's what I'm going to do. And I swear to
you that I will wear this uniform until I walk down the aisle.

RITA   You're crazy . . . you don't know what you're saying!

DON MANUEL   Another one of your whims, Dorotea?

DOROTEA   Well, that's what I'm going to do. I'm going to look for another
bridegroom right now on Main Street. And I promise you that I'll
come back with one. If not this morning, this afternoon. If not today,
tomorrow. But I'll be back for the ceremony. Tell the priest to wait
for me. Tell everyone to wait, that I'll be there . . .

RITA   You're going to look ridiculous, Dorotea!

DOROTEA   Don't I already look ridiculous? Isn't everyone going to laugh
anyway? Wasn't the boy who brought the letter laughing? Well, I'm
going to laugh too . . . walking down the street in my white dress,
looking for another bridegroom . . . they'll see that I'm not afraid of
them, that I'm strong, that their comments and their laughter are not
important to me. And we'll see who is laughing at whom.

RITA   You can't be so foolish . . . you have to accept your fate.

DOROTEA   I am who I am, and there's nothing more to say.

DON MANUEL   Dorotea!

DOROTEA   Don't worry, Papa. I'll be back soon. Give me a kiss . . . and
you too, Aunt Rita. And you, Rosa. Anyway, what I'm going to do is
not so strange. It's what I've always done . . . I'm going for a walk
down Main Street.   [*And with an anguish she tries to hide, she exits
left.*]

CURTAIN

Scene 2

*The scene takes place in Alameda Park, facing the sea (which we imagine
to be in the orchestra of the theater); there are two benches facing the audience, one right, the other left. Between them, downstage, a small railing. In
the background is a garden. It is dusk; from the distance can be heard music
and the sounds of a festival. As the curtain rises, the stage is empty. Juan
Bermúdez enters right. He is thirty-five years old, attractive; he is wearing a
checkered shirt, no tie, a felt hat. He is whistling a light melody; he looks
toward the sea, leans for a moment on the railing, and then sits down on the
left bench, where he continues whistling. Dorotea enters left, still in her wedding dress which is now a little crumpled. She is carrying a furled umbrella
and walks past Juan, who looks surprised. Dorotea greets him and then leans
against the railing.*

DOROTEA   Good evening.

JUAN   Good evening.

DOROTEA   [*After looking toward the sea.*]   Look at that tiny boat! Do you see it?

JUAN   Yes.

DOROTEA   Poor little thing! All alone in the middle of the ocean...the weather's much better today.   [*Juan looks at her without speaking.*]   Why are you staring at me?

JUAN   Sorry...what are you dressed as?

DOROTEA   A bride. I've been wearing this for seven months.

JUAN   Ah!

DOROTEA   In August, God willing, it will be a year.   [*She sits down on the right bench.*]   You're a stranger, aren't you?

JUAN   Yes, I own the merry-go-round at the fair.

DOROTEA   And why aren't you running it?

JUAN   Because it's broken. I'm waiting for a new part from Madrid.

DOROTEA   I see.

JUAN   Listen, why are you dressed like a bride? Some sort of joke?

DOROTEA   No, I'm dressed this way because my fiancé left me, and I'm looking for a replacement.

JUAN   Of course. Naturally. Tell me, are there many like you in this town or are you the only one?

DOROTEA   All the women in this town are crazy. But the same thing is true in Philadelphia...it's not a question of geography but of sensibility.

JUAN   [*Ready to agree to anything.*]   If you say so.

DOROTEA   After all, the fact that I am dressed this way doesn't prove I'm crazy. If it did, soldiers—or anyone who wore a uniform—would be crazy. I wear the uniform of a bride, and that's all. I'm in the service.

JUAN   Of course.

DOROTEA   That's what's wrong with you strangers—you're shocked by anything new.

JUAN   That may be.

DOROTEA   And you're probably from Madrid!

JUAN   Well, yes...I am.

DOROTEA   I thought so. You people always think you know so much—when you know nothing! Every Sunday you have to go to the country...how routine!

JUAN   That's true.   [*He smiles, beginning to like her.*]

DOROTEA   All our visitors, except those from Bayonne, are idiots! An English journalist who came through reported in the London papers that all Spanish women walked down the street in wedding dresses, playing castanets and with a priest at their side. What a fool!   [*She *gets up and leans on the railing.*]   Look, that tiny boat! How far out it is!

JUAN   It's moving very fast.

DOROTEA   Ships don't move, they sail. Don't be so stupid.

JUAN   [*Moving toward her.*]   Excuse me.

DOROTEA   You're excused.

JUAN   Tell me, if you're not crazy, why are you dressed like that?

DOROTEA   I've already told you. Because my fiancé left me on the way to the altar.

JUAN   But this has happened to others, and they haven't acted this way.

DOROTEA   That's because they had no pride or dignity. And because they weren't rebels, like me.

JUAN   Ah, I didn't know that.

DOROTEA   Well, I am. Very much of one. But the problem is that this rebel business is not only making me look ridiculous, I'm not enjoying it.

JUAN   I'm not surprised.

DOROTEA   Do you know why?

JUAN   I've no idea.

DOROTEA   Because, clearly, being a rebel is useless. No one understands heroic gestures. Originality itself is disappearing. And they've won. The conformists...

JUAN   Yes.

DOROTEA   You don't understand anything I'm saying, do you?

JUAN   Actually, very little...

DOROTEA   Would you like to sit down?

JUAN   Very much.

DOROTEA   Let's sit here...   [*Dorotea sits down on the bench, left and Juan sits by her. When she begins speaking, José Rivadavia enters upstage right. He is about forty years old and dressed carelessly, perhaps needs a shave. Nevertheless, despite neglect in appearance, he is clearly a gentleman. Although they are unaware of it, he is interested in the couple on the bench and is listening to their conversation. After a short while, he exits left.*]   Well, I'll explain it to you. When my fiancé left me because of the gossip in the town, I wanted to make some valiant and heroic gesture. I said to myself: "So Fermín has walked out on me and everyone is going to make a joke of it. I can't have that. I'll be the one who laughs at them." And so I wore my wedding dress out on the street, looking for another bridegroom. Everyone was waiting in the church...I couldn't think of anything that seemed more logical...

JUAN   Of course.

DOROTEA   I went to Main Street, which for us is a sort of Persian Bazaar where matters of the heart are negotiated. Since there was no one there because it was very early, and it was raining, it occurred to me to go to Dionisio's house...he's a suitor who wanted to marry me so he could expand his business. I explained to him what had happened and suggested he put on a dark suit and come to the church so we could be married. He looked at me, astonished, and said, "Well, the truth is, this is so sudden...I have a previous appointment with a salesman from Sabadell..." Just excuses. "All right," I said to him, "don't worry. I'll find someone else." And I went back to Main Street. And met another. And another. And nothing. Everybody thought I was crazy and tried to avoid me. In the meantime, everybody was telling me what to do...my friends, who came and went daily...my papa, out-of-sorts. My aunt, griping at everyone...the priests... the mayor...*all* of them. And I wouldn't give in. I was not going to take off that dress. I'd sworn I wouldn't, and I wasn't going to do it. I got home late that night without having found a solution. I was tired, defeated...and with the whole town against me.

JUAN   I can imagine.

DOROTEA   But the worst was yet to come.

JUAN   What happened?

DOROTEA   The next day I had to make the big decision. On waking, I asked myself, "Well, are you going to put that dress on or not?" Because, obviously, if I put on a skirt and blouse and went out as usual—or if I stayed home, crying—what purpose would my grand gesture of the day before have served? None. It would have been totally ridiculous. And so I decided that what I needed to do was to continue, so they would have to face the consequences of their gossip and criticism. I would become the ghost of their conscience. Do you like that phrase?

JUAN   Very much.   [*Upstage, left, Rivadavia appears again; he repeats the same pattern as before, disappears left.*]

DOROTEA   And so I did. I put on my wedding dress and once again went out into the street. And once again, the scandal, the laughter, the weeping, the whole thing...and the next day, all over again.   [*She gets up and goes to the railing.*]   My father died the following month. And still I continued. It was hard, but I did it. It was like one of those things that you get into and then can't get out of. It was a question of pride, of stubbornness, of being a spoiled brat...it was a matter of who was going to laugh at whom. Who was the strongest? Who would win? And I didn't find anyone who would marry me, so they won and I lost. But still, I can't back down. You understand?

JUAN   More or less.

DOROTEA   At any rate, I'm tired...it's been so many months...if it just didn't rain... to be dressed like this in this weather... [*She listens for the wind.*] Do you notice how the wind changes? When it comes from the northeast, we can hear the music from the fair... when it shifts to the south, we can't...

JUAN   Tell me something... forgive me, but why didn't they lock you up somewhere?

DOROTEA   Because I'm the richest person in town, and because my father was important. Still, even he had to pay a hundred peseta fine because of the public scandal. If I had been poor, I'd be rotting in jail.

JUAN   But isn't it time to take that dress off?

DOROTEA   I can't—until I get married. I haven't told you the most important part. I promised my father, may he rest in peace... I swore to him... and I have to keep my promise.

JUAN   You could get married.

DOROTEA   Not now. Anyone who would marry me would do it out of pity, which I don't want... anyway, who would dare to marry the town madwoman?

JUAN   But you say that you're not...

DOROTEA   Actually, I'm no longer sure that's true. Perhaps everything I've told you is only the justification that I myself created. Who knows, I may be completely mad. And what you've just heard may be the tale of an idiot told by the protagonist... [*Rosa enters right.*]

ROSA   Señorita Dorotea!

DOROTEA   Hello, Rosa.

ROSA   What are you doing here? I've been looking everywhere...

DOROTEA   I've been telling this man my life story... what's your name?

JUAN   Juan.

DOROTEA   [*Introducing them.*]   This is Juan... and this is Rosa...

ROSA   How do you do...

JUAN   Pleased to meet you...

ROSA   It's getting a little cool, Señorita... we ought to go home...

DOROTEA   Nonsense, it's still early.

ROSA   Your aunt was asking about you. She sent me to look for you...

DOROTEA   Let her wait...

ROSA   But we can't. There are strangers in town for the fair... they might...

DOROTEA   This man is a stranger, and he hasn't done anything. Have you?

JUAN   What?

DOROTEA   See?

ROSA   But Señorita...

DOROTEA   Please, Rosa... leave me alone. Just wait here until I get back.

ROSA   Where are you going?

DOROTEA   To take a walk.

ROSA   Let me come with you.

DOROTEA   No, Rosa, stay here and I'll come by for you later. You know I like to walk alone to show everyone how brave I am...that I don't care about what they say. Good-bye, Señor. Thank you for listening to me. You've been very kind.   [*Dorotea exits right. When she has gone, Rosa sits down on the right bench and talks to Juan.*]

ROSA   Why did you come here?

JUAN   I was just out for a walk.

ROSA   But why were you talking to her?

JUAN   I was just sitting here and she came up and started talking. I couldn't ignore her. Anyhow, it's not important...   [*He sits down next to her.*]

ROSA   But it is. Because when I arrived and saw you together, I didn't know what to do. I didn't know whether to say we knew each other...have you told her anything?

JUAN   No. Why should I? Since you don't want...

ROSA   I feel funny telling her about us...not because she'd care...in fact, she's always after me to find a boyfriend and get married. But with the way things are, I don't feel right. What did she tell you?

JUAN   Her story. More or less what you told me.

ROSA   What do you think of her?

JUAN   What should I think? At times I couldn't tell if she was serious or joking. But the truth is, she's crazy...don't you think so?

ROSA   I'm just not sure because this whole thing with the townspeople is so confusing. I'm not very worldly, and I don't understand why people do what they do. The only thing I know is that she's good to me. And that I'm the only one she has left, because, little by little, all of her friends have abandoned her. They've never really liked her anyway, and now...after all this...

JUAN   But she *is* rich?

ROSA   Oh yes. Half the town is hers. And the meat markets. And the wine shop. And the hotel and restaurant at the station, where we're living.

JUAN   With all that money, she can find someone else to take care of her.

ROSA   [*Gets up and goes to the railing.*]   She doesn't need care...she's not sick. She needs companionship and love and someone who understands her. I understand her, and we get along.

JUAN   What are we going to do then?

ROSA   Do? About what?

JUAN   About our situation.

ROSA   What is our situation?

JUAN   What do you mean? I want to go on seeing you. But not like this...I'm serious about you.   [*He moves toward her.*]

ROSA   That's funny.

JUAN   What's funny?

ROSA   We've only known each other three days! And all we've done is talk a little in the evenings...

JUAN   And kissed.

ROSA   So what? In little towns, we do a lot of kissing.

JUAN   And you do it so well!   [*He puts his arms around her.*]

ROSA   We learn kissing at the edge of town at dusk...in the open so we can't go too far...I've heard that in Paris they don't kiss nearly as much. Everyone is too busy and in too much of a hurry...they always have to take a trolley or the subway, so they don't have time for that. Here we have plenty of time. And we use it for kissing...

JUAN   I'm really fond of you. And I want to marry you. And take you to Madrid...

ROSA   Don't talk about getting married. Or Madrid. Anyway, you'll be leaving town as soon as the fair is over.

JUAN   [*Detaining her.*]   Listen to me!

ROSA   No, I don't want to hear any more...I'm in a hurry.

JUAN   Okay, but give me a kiss.

ROSA   Of course.   [*They kiss.*]   Did you like it?

JUAN   A lot.

ROSA   So did I. Good-bye.   [*Rosa exits right. Juan looks after her. José Rivadavia enters left and comes up to Juan; he also watches her leave.*]

JOSÉ   What a woman!

JUAN   Yes, she is!

JOSÉ   And friendly.

JUAN   Very. Were you listening earlier?

JOSÉ   To Señorita Dorotea?

JUAN   Yes.

JOSÉ   I heard bits and pieces.

JUAN   Did you see her?

JOSÉ   Yes. And I think she saw me.

JUAN   When?

JOSÉ   I think she caught a glimpse of me when I walked by.

JUAN   Well?

JOSÉ   Well what?

JUAN   What do you think, Don José?

JOSÉ   I don't know, Bermúdez.

JUAN   What do you mean you don't know? It couldn't be better. Half the town is hers. The restaurant. The meat markets...cattle...

JOSÉ   That's true...

JUAN   And you've seen her...mad as a hatter...

JOSÉ   No.

JUAN   What do you mean, no?

JOSÉ   She's not, Bermúdez. She makes complete sense...she presents her case...she laughs at herself. Painfully, but she laughs. I don't believe she's crazy.

JUAN   How can you say that?

JOSÉ   Because I've seen her. She pretends to be mad, but she's not. Now then, why does she do this? What is she trying to accomplish? What is she hiding? I don't know, Bermúdez. There's something strange here...

JUAN   Listen, Don José, don't tell me that. I've been watching her since I got into town. I've questioned the maid. And the neighbors. And you heard the conversation I just had with her. I'm telling you, she's completely mad. Do you think for a minute I'd have asked you to come all the way from Madrid otherwise? What we need now is a good plan; people in little towns are very suspicious. You'll come up with something.

JOSÉ   If it's as good a deal as you say, why haven't you proposed to *her* instead of to the maid?

JUAN   Because I couldn't pull it off, Don José. What we need is a person with your gift of speech...your art...your abilities. And your style...

JOSÉ   [*He looks at him for a moment.*]   Think of it, Bermúdez. You, who once represented the Rivadavia Opera Company, now touring small towns with a merry-go-round and dedicating yourself to the conquest of domestic servants!

JUAN   What else is there to do? No one wants to hear us anymore...

JOSÉ   [*Indignantly.*]   Don't say that!

JUAN   [*Submissive.*]   All right.

JOSÉ   And that I, the great baritone José Rivadavia, star of his own opera company, has an agent who, though I haven't worked for four years, can only suggest that I come to some small town and marry a woman whose mental faculties are questionable...it's enough to make the gods weep! How could I have fallen so low, Bermúdez?

JUAN   Come on, Don José, it's not that bad. I thought this might interest you. You can't spend the rest of your life sitting in a cafe discussing *The Merry Widow.*

JOSÉ   What I want to do is to find honest work. Practice my profession. I'm not a con man, even if lately it's been a way to survive...

JUAN   But if this turns out right, we could start all over. Because there's real money here...

JOSÉ   But she's not mad, Bermúdez. Part of what she says might be true, but there's something she's hiding. Something mysterious in the past...something...I don't know what, but it's there.

JUAN   You've been in so many operettas that anything seems possible. If wearing a wedding dress for seven months just on a whim isn't...

JOSÉ   I tell you, there could be other reasons.

JUAN   Such as?

JOSÉ   Such as the fact that she was very much in love with the fiancé who left her. And she doesn't want to marry anyone else. And so she's pretending to be mad. Everything about her suggests a hopeless romantic...the last romantic! Whose romanticism is disguised by the dress she wears...

JUAN   You're making things too complicated, Don José.

JOSÉ   There could be other reasons too. There are subtle forces in these small towns...selfish interests...why didn't the family stop her when she first put on the dress? Why weren't they able to prevent this whole thing? Also, Bermúdez, the situation is tricky. How would I meet her? I can't just go up to her and say, I love you very much, will you marry me?

JUAN   Of course not. That's not what I meant.

JOSÉ   There probably have been others who wanted to take advantage...

JUAN   I'm sure there have. Rosa told me she's run into some.

JOSÉ   We have to come up with a foolproof plan. And not just for her, but for the family, the mayor, the priest – the whole town. And I'll really have to marry her, Bermúdez. In the church. As God ordains. Nothing phony.

JUAN   Of course.

JOSÉ   And then what?

JUAN   That's easy. Either before or after, you tell her she has to put all her money and possessions in your name. And after a while, you sell them on the sly and leave for Madrid. Or form a new company...

JOSÉ   That would be rotten.

JUAN   I know. But what else can we do? This is a crisis in the arts.

JOSÉ   And what are you planning to do? Marry the other one?

JUAN   If there's no other way, I will. As long as I can go when you do, it'll be all right...

JOSÉ   Tell me something, Bermúdez. When you were my agent, were you always such a scoundrel?

JUAN   More or less.

JOSÉ   I'm not surprised we went broke...

JUAN   Well yes, Don José...but to get back to our plan...

JOSÉ   I don't know. I'll have to think about it. I'll have to go back to

Madrid in order to return here . . . because I have to win her properly, romantically, as she deserves . . .

JUAN   You do see it as a business transaction?

JOSÉ   At this moment I see it as a plan to save a woman . . . the ocean, you know, is very near . . . and I didn't like the way she was looking out to sea. Can you lend me a little cash for expenses?

JUAN   [*He looks toward the right.*]   Yes . . . but we better go . . . I think I hear them.

JOSÉ   Why are they coming back?

JUAN   I don't know.

JOSÉ   We can't let them see us together. Let's go.

JUAN   This way, Don José. . . .   [*They exit left. The music from the fair is heard more distinctly. Rosa enters right followed by Dorotea.*]

ROSA   See, there's no one here.

DOROTEA   But I saw him here a minute ago, talking with someone. And I wondered who it was.

ROSA   Probably some friend. He's from Madrid and there are a lot of visitors here for the fair.

DOROTEA   So you really do like him?

ROSA   He's all right. He seems rather nice . . . he owns the merry-go-round and he told me, if I wanted to, he'd sell it so we could get married . . .

DOROTEA   Then do it at once. I'll help you with anything you need.

ROSA   One of my friends told me I shouldn't marry him. She said he wasn't right for me . . . that he was probably unreliable . . .

DOROTEA   Don't pay any attention to anything your friends say or anyone else. If you like him, do it. Go ahead and marry him . . . and leave this town. The sooner the better.

ROSA   Why do you say that?

DOROTEA   Because they'll hurt you, as they have me.

ROSA   You brought it on yourself because you wanted . . .

DOROTEA   [*After a pause.*]   If only you knew!

ROSA   What?

DOROTEA   Many things. But they're things that I don't want to talk about. I don't want even to think about them. I want to forget them.

ROSA   I don't understand.

DOROTEA   [*Looks at the sea.*]   The fishing boats are coming in.

ROSA   Yes.

DOROTEA   [*She is listening.*]   Do you hear? It's pretty, isn't it . . . the music from the fair. It seems to be calling to us, urging us to join in.

ROSA   Let's go then, if you want.

DOROTEA   No, not today.

ROSA   Why not?

DOROTEA   Somehow today I'm ashamed to be seen like this.

ROSA   [*Hopeful.*]   Let's go home then. You can change your dress and then we'll go. We'll ride the merry-go-round. And the other carousel...and we'll have something to drink and see everybody... and maybe talk to Juan...and laugh...and then this will all be over.

DOROTEA   I can't, Rosa. I made a promise. Come on, let's go.

ROSA   Where are we going?

DOROTEA   Where we always go, Rosa. To take our customary stroll down Main Street.   [*They slowly exit left while the music gets louder.*]

CURTAIN

ACT TWO

Scene 1

*A bar in the restaurant in the train station. Downstage left is a door;
over it is a sign which reads, "Entrance to the Restaurant." Upstage is a
counter and back of it, a wall with rows of bottles. In the rear wall are large
doubledoors that lead to the station platform. Through the glass in the doors
we see, at one point, the lights of one of the trains that passes. Right center
there is another door, also with windows, that leads to outside (but not to the
platform). Scattered about are three or four tables with chairs. Two of these
tables are downstage: one on the right, one left. There are large flower pots,
coatracks, and posters on the wall advertising mineral water and aperitifs.
There is a large round clock that reads 7:50, and it is beginning to get dark.
As the curtain rises, we see Inés, Benita, and Remedios seated at the table to
the right. They are serious and tense, obviously waiting for someone. They
all have umbrellas. We can hear the wind. The curtains blow. After a minute, Inés sneezes.*

INÉS   Achew!
REMEDIOS   Bless you.
INÉS   Thank you.
REMEDIOS   You're welcome.
INÉS   I've caught it!
BENITA   I'm not surprised, with this weather.
INÉS   And I'm dressed warmly.
REMEDIOS   I am too, but it doesn't help here. Especially in early
    spring.   [*The station bell rings loudly.*]
BENITA   Is it time for the train?
REMEDIOS   [*Looking at the clock on the wall.*]   No. Nothing arrives until
    the mail train at 8:15.
INÉS   What bell is that?
REMEDIOS   The one on the platform.
BENITA   Why is it ringing?
REMEDIOS   It's not ringing. The wind is blowing it.
INÉS   Some wind!
BENITA   Yes, it's really blowing.
REMEDIOS   It's from the northeast.
BENITA   It blew my brother away again today.
INÉS   Again?
BENITA   Again.

REMEDIOS   I don't know why you let him go out on the balcony when he's so sickly.

BENITA   Well, you let your father get water from the well and he's sickly, too.

REMEDIOS   It's Mama who lets him do that. She does it on purpose because she's never really liked him.

INÉS   I know. Moreover, your mother has always been mean.

REMEDIOS   It's the humidity that affects her.

INÉS   Was the child hurt?

BENITA   Who knows? It was such a strong gust we haven't found him yet.

REMEDIOS   Isn't that the same thing that happened to the other one?

BENITA   The very same...it's a shame.   [*From within, a strident whistle.*]

INÉS   What was that? The wind again?

REMEDIOS   No, it's the coffee pot in the restaurant.

INÉS   What a confusing station. Someday there's going to be a catastrophe.

BENITA   I know.   [*She looks at the clock.*]

INÉS   Obviously.   [*Looks at the clock also.*]

REMEDIOS   You know they're making us wait on purpose.

INÉS   Yes, it's intentional.

REMEDIOS   I can't imagine they have much business.

INÉS   On a day like this! There's not even a stray cat in the restaurant.

BENITA   You know, the one they had died of food poisoning.

REMEDIOS   One day he got careless and tried something from the menu.

INÉS   And they say the trains are always late...

BENITA   What really happens is that trains don't come down this track until the engineer sees that the restaurant is closed.

REMEDIOS   That's so the passengers won't try to order...and have something terrible happen.

INÉS   I'll bet they tell us the restaurant was full of people.

BENITA   I think they suspect what we're here for and they're afraid.

INÉS   They should be. This is a serious problem.

BENITA   It's a problem they deserve.

INÉS   Actually, I'm beginning to feel bad about this.

BENITA   Don't be foolish; our future is at stake.

REMEDIOS   This is not something to take lightly, Inés.

BENITA   We have to protect ourselves, whatever the cost.

REMEDIOS   And whoever is hurt.   [*Rosa enters through the restaurant door. She is carrying a tray and is wearing a white apron, like a waitress. She goes toward the counter, turns on the lights, and looks for a bottle and some glasses while she speaks.*]

ROSA   She'll be right here.

REMEDIOS   Thank you.

ROSA   She said she's sorry to keep you waiting so long.

BENITA   It's quite all right.

INÉS   We know she's very busy.

ROSA   Oh, no. She doesn't have anything to do. Right now she's just getting ready to go out. She told me to invite you to have something to
drink. Let me pour you some wine.

REMEDIOS   No, thanks. We'd rather not have anything here.

BENITA   Don't bother.

INÉS   Please don't!

ROSA   [*Showing them a bottle that she's going to open.*]   Don't be nervous. This is real wine and I'm going to open a new bottle just for
you...look...it's never been touched. See?

BENITA   Well, in that case...

ROSA   [*While she's opening the bottle.*]   This is not what we give the
tourists. Not at all. Why should we give good wine to someone who
will never be back? Because they never are. I've never seen the same
person twice. They arrive, get off the train, order, sneeze. Two minutes later, the whistle blows and they leave...good-bye...and we
never see them again. It's as if the earth had swallowed them
up.   [*She serves the wine.*]   You'll like this...

INÉS   Thank you.

BENITA   Thank you.

REMEDIOS   How are you and your boyfriend getting along?

ROSA   Fine. He's down at the merry-go-round...

BENITA   You must be very happy.

ROSA   Yes, I am. He's very good to me. I've always wanted to have a real
boyfriend, haven't you?

INÉS   Perhaps.

REMEDIOS   Does he want to marry you or is he just after the same old
thing?

ROSA   He says both: first one and then the other.

BENITA   They all say that. But they all want to *start* with the same old
thing.

ROSA   Well, what difference does it make? The order of the factors
doesn't alter the product.

REMEDIOS   Just be careful you don't end up nursing the product.

ROSA   We all give what we have the most of. Especially if there's more
than enough. Of course, it's not the same for everyone...enjoy the
wine...excuse me...   [*She exits left.*]

INÉS   Well, I expected her to be snippier.

BENITA   She wouldn't dare.

REMEDIOS   Ever since she's had this boyfriend she's been insufferable.

INÉS   Does Doña Rita know about all this?

REMEDIOS   Yes, she does. He comes to the house and everything. I'm
telling you, they're going to get married.

BENITA   Well, she is cute. But...

INÉS   I don't know what he sees in her.

REMEDIOS   Probably just what he's looking for.

BENITA   I don't think so. Rosa is a tease, but I don't think it goes...
[*Doña Rita enters left. She is dressed in black and is wearing a coat,
clearly ready to go out. The three friends get up when she comes in.*]

RITA   Good afternoon.

THE THREE WOMEN   Good afternoon.

RITA   How nice to see you here...after all this time.

REMEDIOS   Well, here we are.

BENITA   It's nice to see you, too.

RITA   Thank you. And your father, Inés? Still so sickly?

INÉS   Yes, Señora. Still the same.

RITA   That's too bad. Maybe it would be better if the good Lord would
take him. And while He's at it, your aunt.

INÉS   But my aunt is fine!

RITA   I just meant so the poor man wouldn't have to go all alone.

INÉS   Oh, yes.

RITA   Ah, Beni. I heard you pushed another brother off the balcony.

BENITA   It was the wind, Doña Rita.

RITA   Aren't people terrible! Everyone is saying it's *you* who's been push-
ing them off, one by one.

BENITA   Just gossip...you know how people are...

RITA   So. Rosa told me you wanted to speak to me?

REMEDIOS   Well, yes. It's a rather delicate matter.

RITA   Please sit down, then.   [*Rita sits next to the table at the left; the
other three sit down.*]

THE THREE WOMEN   Thank you.

RITA   You were saying...

BENITA   This morning we went to see the Mayor...

RITA   How nice!

INÉS   We went as a group.

BENITA   Seven young ladies from the town...

REMEDIOS   And at the head of the group was Pepita Rodríguez, who is
our president.

INÉS   And you know how powerful Pepita Rodríguez is.

RITA   She must have taken some cod-liver oil, because she used to be
quite puny.

REMEDIOS   We weren't talking about her physical strength – everybody
knows she's hopelessly skinny – but her influence.

BENITA   After all, next to Dorotea, she's the richest woman in town...

REMEDIOS   Anyway, at the end of the meeting, the Mayor, who knows that we're friends of Dorotea's, asked us to talk to her. Or to you...

RITA   To tell me what?

INÉS   First of all, the Mayor has agreed to what we've planned for the summer if the weather permits.

REMEDIOS   We're not only going to have fireworks and a puppet show, but also a greased pole.

BENITA   And we're going to dance in the Casino until dawn.

REMEDIOS   And on Main Street we're going to string colored lights from one balcony to the next...one blue bulb, then a green one, then a red...

BENITA   And another red, another green, another blue.

REMEDIOS   All over the place.

INÉS   Imagine the effect!

REMEDIOS   And a lot of other simple, smalltown attractions that will appeal not only to people from Madrid and Zaragoza, but even foreign countries. They'll be as thick as flies...

BENITA   Today we've begun Novenas asking God that it not rain... [*To Doña Rita, who is looking distracted.*]   Are you listening, Doña Rita?

RITA   I am...but I'm not sure God is...look at the weather.

INÉS   But it will change! Any day now, when we least expect it, the sun is going to come out!

RITA   Very well, what else? Get to the point.

REMEDIOS   Well, in conclusion, the group decided—and the Mayor agreed with us—to put an end to the humiliation and embarrassment that Dorotea's shameful attitude has created in our town.

BENITA   At first, we just laughed at her behavior, and then we felt sorry for her. But now, everybody is getting sick of it.

INÉS   She not only makes herself look ridiculous, but the rest of us as well.

REMEDIOS   Wandering down Main Street in that white dress, she's as familiar as one of the beggars—only instead of a sign saying, "I need bread," she seems to be saying, "I need a man."

INÉS   It's as if she's focusing attention on all the other women in town who need a husband—but suffer in silence.

BENITA   Surely you can understand that we can't put up with this situation any longer.

REMEDIOS   It's for the good of the whole town, Doña Rita.

INÉS   Our fishing industry shouldn't have to pay because Dorotea was jilted...

RITA   You have to remember she promised her father.

REMEDIOS   It was a promise made in a moment of passion and grief.

BENITA   Anyway, the promise was just that she would be married in the dress she was wearing. And she's had chances to do that.

INÉS   Somebody agreed to marry her only four months ago.

RITA   But he was ancient!

REMEDIOS   She can't be choosy.

BENITA   And there was another one who was willing to sacrifice himself.

RITA   [*Gets up.*]   It's not a question of sacrifice or any of this other gibberish! With all her defects and peculiarities, Dorotea is still Dorotea. And I will not consent to having my niece marry a nobody in order to save the town some embarrassment. It's true that a few have offered to marry her for her money. And some out of pity, but who were they? Upstarts, without a cent to their name. And she *is* my niece so I must look out for her. I'm constantly sacrificing myself, working my fingers to the bone to protect her interests.

REMEDIOS   In other words, you're not going to help us.

RITA   What do you have in mind?

BENITA   Couldn't you at least keep her at home . . . so she doesn't wander the streets like a madwoman?

RITA   I can't stop her. You know how she is.

REMEDIOS   All right then, Doña Rita. We hate to say this, but the Mayor has decided to put an end to this: he's not going to tolerate her running loose any more. Dorotea, poor dear, is crazy. And so he's going to have her committed.

RITA   This can't be! It's not true!

BENITA   He's already talked to the Governor . . .

INÉS   And you have to be the one to tell Dorotea . . .

REMEDIOS   If she has any sanity left, maybe she'll stop . . .

BENITA   And we won't have to go to these extremes . . . which we all hate . . .

REMEDIOS   You know how distasteful this is . . . we're her friends and we love her . . .

INÉS   But something has to be done.

RITA   [*Pensively.*]   Yes, I see. Of course . . .

BENITA   We can count on you?

RITA   I'll tell her what's happened. And I'll try again, as I have before, to get her to be reasonable . . . but if she's mad, as you say . . .

REMEDIOS   We'll come back tomorrow for an answer.

INÉS   We're very sorry, Doña Rita.

RITA   That's all right.

BENITA   Thank you for everything . . .

RITA   Thank you for telling me.

REMEDIOS   I hope everything will be all right.

RITA   I'll do what I can.

INÉS   We know you will.

REMEDIOS   Good-bye, then.

BENITA   Please give her our regards...

RITA   Of course. [*During the farewell, the three have been moving toward the right door.*]

INÉS   Good-bye, Doña Rita.

RITA   Good-bye, dears.

THE THREE WOMEN   Good-bye.

RITA   Until tomorrow. [*They exit right. Rita sees them out and continues standing by the door. Dorotea, still in her wedding dress and holding some flowers, enters left.*]

DOROTEA   Were those my friends?

RITA   [*Closing the door.*]   Yes, your friends.

DOROTEA   Rosa just told me. What did they want?

RITA   To tell me about the festival plans for the coming season.

DOROTEA   Was that all?

RITA   Yes.

DOROTEA   I'd like to have seen them.

RITA   Why? You know how they feel about you.

DOROTEA   Still, since they were here, you might have told me. Perhaps we might have become friends again, as we used to be... and talked together...

RITA   Don't you think it would be better if you went for a walk instead of being stuck in the house all day?

DOROTEA   Outside?

RITA   Of course...to get some fresh air...as you used to...

DOROTEA   I don't feel like it today. I don't know why, but I'm beginning to be embarrassed to have people see me this way.

RITA   The townspeople? As if you cared what they say! What are you doing with those flowers?

DOROTEA   I picked them in the garden to put on the tables. Summer is almost here and we need to decorate so the tourists will feel like coming in. I'm going to put them in vases and set one on each table.

RITA   [*Indicating the glasses left on the table at the right.*]   Would you mind picking up those glasses?

DOROTEA   No, of course not. [*She leaves the flowers on the table and collects the glasses.*]

RITA   I'm going to the wine shop to do the weekly accounts with Andrés. We have a lot to do today. I'll get Rosa to come and keep you company.

DOROTEA   If you like...

RITA   [*Going to the door on the left.*]   Until later, then.

DOROTEA   Listen, Aunt Rita...

RITA   [*She returns.*]   What?

DOROTEA   My friends...all they wanted was to talk about the festival?

RITA   That's all. What else would they want?

DOROTEA   That's true. There's nothing else...and Andrés?

RITA   Andrés?

DOROTEA   Yes. How is he?

RITA   He's fine, Dorotea. He's a big help to me. If it weren't for him...

DOROTEA   I understand...until later, Aunt Rita.

RITA   Good-bye, Dorotea.

> [*Rita exits left, while Dorotea goes behind the counter—which thus
> hides part of her dress—and puts down the glasses. After her aunt has
> gone, she remains thoughtful, and her sad smile indicates that she has
> understood everything. At this moment, José Rivadavia enters right.
> He is in a tuxedo and top hat; his apparel is a little worn and wrinkled.
> He also carries a suitcase that is worn; his expression is smiling, pleas-
> ant, and theatrical.*]

JOSÉ   May I come in?

DOROTEA   [*Surprised.*]   What?

JOSÉ   I said, may I come in?

DOROTEA   Yes...come in.

JOSÉ   [*Taking off his hat.*]   Good evening, Señorita.

DOROTEA   Good evening, Señor.

JOSÉ   Is this the train station?

DOROTEA   The restaurant in the station.

JOSÉ   Do you know how long it will be before the next train?

DOROTEA   What train?

JOSÉ   I don't care...any train...the next one that comes through.

DOROTEA   I think the express is due.

JOSÉ   [*Pleased.*]   Is that right?

DOROTEA   Yes, it's time for it.

JOSÉ   What great luck!

DOROTEA   But it doesn't stop here. It goes right by, like so many
others...

JOSÉ   That's even better.

DOROTEA   Why better?

JOSÉ   All I want to do is wave to the passengers and wish them a good
trip. Since I can't be happy myself, at least I can wish happiness for
others.

DOROTEA   In that case, this is the train for you.

JOSÉ   How do I get to the platform?

DOROTEA   [*Pointing to the door.*]   Just go through that door.

JOSÉ   Does it open out or in?

DOROTEA   In.

JOSÉ   Like this?

DOROTEA   Like that.

JOSÉ   Thank you very much, Señorita.

DOROTEA   You're quite welcome, Señor.

JOSÉ   Good-bye.

DOROTEA   Good-bye.   [*José exits upstage. Dorotea comes from behind the counter and goes toward the door, left.*]   Rosa! Come here! Quickly! [*Rosa enters.*]

ROSA   What's the matter?

DOROTEA   A man just came in!

ROSA   In where?

DOROTEA   Here. And then he went out on the platform.

ROSA   So?

DOROTEA   But he's not like the rest. He's like me!   [*She points to her temple to indicate he is mad.*]

ROSA   I don't understand.   [*Dorotea goes toward the upstage door and opens it a little.*]

DOROTEA   Look. Do you see him?

ROSA   [*Looking.*]   A senator!

DOROTEA   No, Rosa. Senators don't wave at trains that aren't passing.

ROSA   It hasn't passed because it's ten minutes late.

DOROTEA   But he's waving.

ROSA   Yes. . .and now he's coming this way.

DOROTEA   I'm going to hide, Rosa.

ROSA   Hide?

DOROTEA   Behind the counter. He didn't notice my dress before, and I don't want him to see it now.   [*She goes behind the counter. José enters again.*]

JOSÉ   The train's already gone. It went so fast I could hardly see the passengers, but I wished them all a good trip anyway. And now I'm content because I'm sure they'll all reach their destination happily.   [*He addresses Rosa, who looks astonished.*]   Were you here before?

ROSA   No, Señor. I just got here.

JOSÉ   I wish you happiness, too.

ROSA   Thank you.

JOSÉ   You're welcome.   [*To Dorotea.*]   This is a nice place to watch the trains go by, don't you think?

DOROTEA   Yes, it is. And there is plenty of time for it.

JOSÉ   When does another one come by?

DOROTEA   The mail train doesn't come through until tomorrow morning. . .

JOSÉ   If I could stay here for the night, I'd like to see it. Besides, I've already sent the limousine away...

ROSA   You came in a limousine?

JOSÉ   I travel everywhere by limousine. Otherwise, the children pester me, you know.

ROSA   Yes.

DOROTEA   There's an inn here...if you want to stay...

JOSÉ   Are there rooms?

DOROTEA   Of course.

JOSÉ   Vacant?

DOROTEA   All of them.

JOSÉ   I can't believe it.

ROSA   Why does it surprise you?

JOSÉ   Not that the rooms are vacant, but that they're available to me. Because for me, all of the rooms in all of the hotels in all of the world are always occupied.

DOROTEA   Why?

JOSÉ   I'm not sure. First they ask me if I've come to dedicate something...a monument, a reservoir, a small fountain...or to lay a cornerstone...or to make a speech. And when I say 'no,' they are surprised. And then they ask if my wife is waiting in the car and we're on our honeymoon. And when I answer that I spent my honeymoon a long time ago, alone, crying, all doors are closed to me...

DOROTEA   I don't understand why, do you, Rosa?

ROSA   No.

JOSÉ   Maybe it's the way I'm dressed.

DOROTEA   Everyone should be able to dress any way they like.

JOSÉ   No, people have very strict ideas about dress. They think that if I wear a tuxedo, I'm crazy – when the truth is that I wear it because I was buried in it.

ROSA   Aren't you alive?

JOSÉ   Physically, I am, since I see and walk and breathe...but I died in this very suit at the door of a church filled with flowers. It was a summer afternoon, warmed by a radiant sun, an afternoon when my bride left me at the altar.   [*Made distraught by this memory, he goes to the table, right, and sits down. Rosa moves toward Dorotea, who continues hiding behind the counter.*]

ROSA   Did you hear that?

DOROTEA   Yes, Rosa. A bridegroom!

ROSA   All dressed and everything!

DOROTEA   Like me.

ROSA   You have to do something.

DOROTEA   What?

ROSA   I don't know...talk to him...come out from behind the counter, let him see you...

DOROTEA   I'm afraid to, Rosa...

ROSA   This is your chance, don't you see? I'm going to leave you alone...I'll go look for Juan. Maybe he'll know what to do...

DOROTEA   All right, Rosa.

ROSA   And I'll be a while, all right? I won't rush back...so you two will have a little time to talk...

DOROTEA   You're right. Go.   [*Rosa goes toward the door to the left, looks at José and Dorotea, and says finally.*]

ROSA   Good luck, Señorita...   [*Exits.*]

JOSÉ   [*Recovering from his melancholy state.*]   Your friend is leaving?

DOROTEA   Yes.

JOSÉ   [*Rising.*]   Aren't you afraid to stay here alone with me? Doesn't it at least surprise you that I'm dressed this way?

DOROTEA   Nothing surprises us anymore in this town, Señor.   [*She comes out from behind the counter.*]   Look at me.

JOSÉ   [*Noticing her wedding dress for the first time.*]   Why are you dressed like that?

DOROTEA   For the same reason you are. I was also left at the altar.

JOSÉ   No!

DOROTEA   Yes...

JOSÉ   When?

DOROTEA   A year ago...August 9.

JOSÉ   It can't be!

DOROTEA   But it is. Just as I said...

JOSÉ   But that's the day it happened to me. That must mean that...

DOROTEA   What?

JOSÉ   I don't know...I was just thinking that since we were both abandoned on the same day, alone and without love, well, perhaps those weddings weren't meant to be. Perhaps *we* were meant to meet now.

DOROTEA   What a lovely thought.

JOSÉ   Yes, it is.

DOROTEA   Won't you sit down?

JOSÉ   Thank you.   [*He sits down at the table to the left, where there are still some of the flowers Dorotea has brought. She takes one and offers it to José.*]

DOROTEA   A flower?

JOSÉ   Thank you, again.   [*He puts the flower in his lapel; meanwhile, Dorotea sits down next to him.*]

DOROTEA   What was her name?

JOSÉ   Cándida.

DOROTEA   Where was she from?

JOSÉ   Salamanca. Why do you ask?

DOROTEA   No reason. Did you love her?

JOSÉ   Very much.

DOROTEA   I loved him, too. More than anyone in the world. We talked and laughed together. It's marvelous to have somebody to talk to. It makes all the difference. That was why I acted the way I did after he left. . . so everyone would leave me alone. . . so I could think of him. Why did you come here?

JOSÉ   I travel everywhere, watching the trains go by. It's the kind of trip we planned for our honeymoon. I've been through France, England, Germany, Italy. . . the city I was most comfortable in was London because no one was surprised by my attire. . . here in Spain, on the other hand, the people are not sympathetic toward affairs of the heart. Ferocious children hunt me with lassos. . .

DOROTEA   Why do you still dress that way?

JOSÉ   For spite. . . for revenge. . . as a rebellion. . . and, to tell you the truth, it bothers me to see you dressed this way too. I thought I had exclusive rights to this form of protest. . .

DOROTEA   You're charming.

JOSÉ   If you say so. . .

DOROTEA   What's your name?

JOSÉ   José Rivadavia. And yours?

DOROTEA   Dorotea.

JOSÉ   Which, reversed, is Teodora.

DOROTEA   That's true. But why do you say that?

JOSÉ   Because the name reminds me of a beautiful and moving poem about a town, a bride, and unrequited love.

DOROTEA   How does it go?

JOSÉ   It's called, "The Suitor." [*He stands up to recite the poem.*]
    He promised to come between 7:00 and 8:00
    To court Teodora, to settle her fate
    By seeking her hand as the eldest of all
    The daughters Heredia. The clock in the hall
    Ticked softly; Teodora soon nervously paced
    Beside her dear mother, whose footsteps she traced.
    How anxious they waited, they waited these two,
    Quite sure he'd be early for this rendevous.
    "Pepito is proper," the daughter explained,
    "He'd never be late." Her mother refrained
    From noting in fact that the clock had struck eight
    Without any suitor's approaching the gate.
    "Let's go a bit higher," she said, all aglow;
    "This balcony, clearly, is simply too low."

The mother agreed and so upstairs they climbed
To stare out at emptiness as the clock chimed.
They looked down Main Street, to left and to right,
Reluctantly climbing up yet one more flight.
Another, another, still higher they crept
Until they arrived at the roof, where she wept
At finding below her the town and the farms
But no man reflecting Pepito's sweet charms.
"This house is too low," Teodora declared,
So up to the sky the whole family repaired
And there from a star the great world they surveyed.
"I'm sure that he'll be here; he's just been delayed,"
Teodora proclaimed as she rocked in her chair.
One year passed, then ten, and a hundred to spare;
Pepito was nowhere, not a trace nor a sign—
Pepito, the darling, had a very smooth line!

DOROTEA   [*Truly entertained.*]   Bravo!

JOSÉ   Thank you.

DOROTEA   That's marvelous. And you recited it quite well...

JOSÉ   You're very kind.

DOROTEA   Can I get you something?

JOSÉ   Not right now. Perhaps later I could have a sandwich?

DOROTEA   Would you like a beer first?

JOSÉ   If it's all the same, I'd prefer a cognac.

DOROTEA   I'll get it.   [*The dialogue continues while she goes to the counter and serves José cognac.*]   Why would a woman abandon such a charming man?

JOSÉ   My charm, apparently, was not enough. Two days before our wedding, she met another man who was both charming and the owner of a business. And you?   [*He goes to the counter and stands facing her.*]

DOROTEA   Town gossip. Envy. And above all, my aunt.

JOSÉ   Your aunt?

DOROTEA   Yes. She's really the one to blame.

JOSÉ   Why did you permit it?

DOROTEA   I just found out four months ago and I'm the only one who knows. She was involved with Andrés, her helper at the market. Now he's in charge...

JOSÉ   Really?

DOROTEA   Yes, I caught them one day—but I pretended not to notice. Since then, I've been thinking about it and I've realized that it was my aunt who was driving away all my suitors.

JOSÉ   Why?

DOROTEA   My father wanted me to get married so that my husband and

I could take over his business. This would have left my aunt at home, knitting. And since she didn't want to stay home and knit, she managed to create situations that would make my suitors abandon me. So, with the help of Andrés, she now has everything.

JOSÉ   But that's terrible!

DOROTEA   Not really. These things happen all the time in little towns. For a pair of pigs and a mule, people here are capable of anything. [*She takes the cognac and goes back to the table on the left. Both of them sit down.*]

JOSÉ   But what about the wedding dress?

DOROTEA   I didn't think about it at the time because I was obsessed. But later I remembered that on the day following the scandal, when I didn't think I could continue wearing the dress, it was my aunt who told me, "Yes, dear, put on your wedding dress and go out into the street to show them." Do you understand? Instead of hiding the dress, she encouraged me. And she's still doing it, so they'll lock me up and she'll be rid of me.

JOSÉ   Why don't you do something about it?

DOROTEA   It's too late. Everyone would think I was lying. There's so much hypocrisy involved and I could never prove anything. Anyway, I don't want to cause her any harm. It's not really her fault—it's Andrés, her helper. The problem is that she's in love and does whatever he tells her to do. You know how someone in love does foolish things. Poor woman! It's a shame.

JOSÉ   But to let them lock you up...

DOROTEA   I don't think it will come to that. And if it does, what does it matter? Perhaps I'd be better off if I were locked up.

JOSÉ   That's absurd, you're not crazy.

DOROTEA   How can you be sure?

JOSÉ   You're simply a very sensitive woman. More sensitive than most. And with enough courage not to conceal it. Perhaps we should get married.

DOROTEA   [*She gets up, startled.*]   You and I?

JOSÉ   Yes. And once married, we could take off these costumes...and be happy...

DOROTEA   Could you be happy here, in this town?

JOSÉ   With you, I could be happy anywhere.

DOROTEA   Actually, if there were no more betrayals of love, no more walking down Main Street to find a husband, it might be pleasant to live here. It's true that here you have to protect yourself from the rain and the waves and the gossip, but that just makes you stronger. And when one day, all of a sudden, the sun comes out, there's not a more beautiful place. Not even Bayonne.

JOSÉ [*Rises and goes toward her.*] That's why I think we should get married. I could be in charge of all your business affairs and protect your interests.

DOROTEA And end up with all my money. And then you could take off. Right?

JOSÉ Why do you say that? I don't understand...

DOROTEA Because three days ago you were in town, wearing a checkered jacket. I saw you. You were down the street, but I saw you.

JOSÉ I don't know what you're talking about.

DOROTEA You were in the park, next to the walkway by the sea, talking to Rosa's young man. And now you turn up here, wearing that suit, in order to get me to swallow this nonsense, as she has done. And, given your smooth tongue, as others will. I'll grant you, it's an ingenious plan...but not a kind one.

JOSÉ [*He lowers his head, defeated.*] I don't know what to say. I was destitute, without a job, without hope....a little like you. I'm really not like this. I'm an artist.

DOROTEA An artist?

JOSÉ Actually, I'm a baritone. But not a very good one. A failed actor. At one time, I was successful and believed I was important. But one day the audience stopped applauding, and my vanity and arrogance kept me from continuing the struggle. I began hiding in cafes and blaming my failure on other people, when I was really responsible. Not long ago, Juan called me—he's not a bad fellow—and told me about you. I found this old jacket and ridiculous hat in a theatre trunk I hadn't pawned, and I thought...but forgive me. Would you like me to go now?

DOROTEA No. We need to get married before you go. I suppose that at least you *are* single?

JOSÉ Single and alone. But now that you know why I've come...

DOROTEA I don't care. I'm sick of this white dress, of this obsession of mine, of walking the streets. I can't do it anymore.

JOSÉ I still think it would be better for me to leave.

DOROTEA Why are you running away now? What are you afraid of? [*José doesn't answer.*] You're not looking at my dress, but at me...at my eyes...

JOSÉ Yes.

DOROTEA As if you really cared...why?

JOSÉ Because all my life, like yours, has been neither happy nor triumphant. And now... [*At this moment, we hear the sound of a train passing by and see the lights reflecting in the window of the door.*]

DOROTEA There's the train.

JOSÉ [*Without moving.*] Yes. The train.

DOROTEA   Aren't you going to watch it go by? Aren't you going to wave at the passengers and wish them a happy trip?

JOSÉ   I'm no longer interested in their happiness, only yours.

DOROTEA   I don't know whether you're lying to me or not. . . but stay.

JOSÉ   I shouldn't do this. You know what I am.

DOROTEA   It doesn't matter why you've come with such a tale. It's a marvelous tale. And you're a marvelous storyteller. . . would you give me a kiss? If you'd like to, of course.

JOSÉ   You know I would.   [*They kiss.*]

DOROTEA   Now unbutton my dress, please.

JOSÉ   Here?

DOROTEA   Yes. Do it slowly. . . as if it were our wedding night. I have to take this off before. . .

JOSÉ   But what if someone comes in. . .

DOROTEA   Since we're both crazy, no one will be surprised.

JOSÉ   [*While be begins to unbutton the dress.*]   All right.

DOROTEA   And you have to promise me that, although in the end you may deceive me, until that time. . . when you leave. . . you won't make me unhappy anymore.   [*She turns and embraces him.*] That you will be good to me. And that we will be happy. I want very much to feel good and to laugh a little and to have a good time.   [*And while she takes refuge in his arms, dreamily, the curtain falls rapidly.*]

SCENE 2

Some small improvements have been made in the set. For example, all the tables are covered with bright tablecloths, and there is a vase of flowers on each one. The shelving with the bottles, which is against the wall behind the counter, is decorated with flags from various countries. There are different curtains covering the glass portion of the rear doors; these changes, including new lights, make the whole set more appealing and pleasant. It's eight o'clock at night and the lights are turned on. As the curtain rises, we see Juan seated at a table to the right. He is dunking a sweet roll in his coffee. As he eats, he looks at his watch and compares the time with that shown on the wall clock. A little later Rosa enters from the door at left. She is carrying a tray with a plate of sweet rolls, and she approaches Juan cheerfully.

ROSA   Juan!

JUAN   Yes.

ROSA   I brought you more rolls.

JUAN   Thank you, my love.

ROSA   You're welcome, my darling.   [*She sits next to him and watches him eat.*]   They're good, aren't they?

JUAN   Very.

ROSA   The Señorita made them. And I helped her.

JUAN   They're delicious.

ROSA   She used to make all kinds of pastry. And special desserts. Cream puffs, eclairs, apple tarts, and I don't know what else. It's been so long I thought she might have forgotten how...but as you can see...

JUAN   No, she hasn't forgotten. These are wonderful...

ROSA   How did you like the *arroz la marinera* that we served for lunch?

JUAN   It was excellent!

ROSA   I made it myself. We're going to get a cook to help us, and soon this place will be full of people. We have three for dinner tonight.

JUAN   Travelers?

ROSA   No, townspeople. They're not afraid to eat here anymore.

JUAN   That's good.   [*He continues eating greedily.*]

ROSA   [*She continues staring at him.*]   I think you've gotten fatter since we got married.

JUAN   I have. It's only been a month and a half, and I've already put on five pounds.   [*He pushes his plate away.*]

ROSA   Good. You look better this way. Can I get you something else?

JUAN   You could pour me a glass of anise, if you wouldn't mind.

ROSA   Of course, Juan. I'll get it.   [*She gets up and goes behind the counter, which gives Juan time to sneak a glance at his watch.*]   Where is Don José?

JUAN   I don't know. I haven't seen him this afternoon. He must have gone out for a walk.

ROSA   Maybe he's at the station, playing dominoes with the chief.

JUAN   No, not today...

ROSA   Why not?

JUAN   [*Barely concealing his irritation.*]   Because, Rosa, he's just not...

ROSA   You seem irritable, Juan.

JUAN   I do?

ROSA   Yes.

JUAN   I don't know why...   [*Rosa serves him the anise; she continues looking at him, trying to conceal her anxiety.*]

ROSA   Here you are.

JUAN   Thanks.   [*He drinks it in one swallow.*]   Do you know if the Madrid train is late?

ROSA   Going or coming?

JUAN   Don't be funny. The one going to Madrid.

ROSA   Why do you ask?

JUAN   No reason. Because it's time, and they haven't announced it.

ROSA   Well, it must be late . . .

JUAN   Where is your Señorita?

ROSA   Some of her friends came to call.

JUAN   The magpies?

ROSA   There's only one magpie left. The other two have found suitors . . .

JUAN   Oh, really?

ROSA   Yes. During the festival. At the greased pole. And they're going to get married . . .

JUAN   [*Distracted.*]   That's nice. Well, I have to go . . .

ROSA   Where are you going?

JUAN   I don't know. Out . . . to the platform.

ROSA   To the platform?

JUAN   Yes. I need a little air.

ROSA   How about a kiss before you go.

JUAN   Why?

ROSA   No reason. I just want one.   [*They kiss.*]

JUAN   Good-bye.

ROSA   Good-bye.   [*Juan exits rear. Rosa watches him leave, concerned. Dorotea enters left, looking very pretty; she is calm and dressed normally. Remedios and Benita follow her. Benita is very different; she is now dreamy and romantic.*]

DOROTEA   Come see how we've fixed this up.

BENITA   Oh, you have! How pretty! . . .

REMEDIOS   Do you like it?

BENITA   It's really pretty!

DOROTEA   Rosa, what are you doing?

ROSA   Oh, nothing. Waiting for the train . . .

REMEDIOS   It's the one from Bilbao. To Madrid, isn't it?

DOROTEA   Yes. The one that stops here for only a minute.

REMEDIOS   [*Sarcastically.*]   Long enough!

DOROTEA   Why do you say that?

REMEDIOS   Oh, no reason. Just because.

DOROTEA   Rosa, would you clear this table, please . . .

ROSA   Of course, Señorita, right away.   [*Rosa collects Juan's dishes and exits right, while Dorotea and her friends continue speaking.*]

BENITA   Dorotea, I really like what you've done. It's lovely. And flowers on all the tables.   [*She takes a flower and smells it.*]

DOROTEA   Flowers . . . curtains . . . new tablecloths . . . and those little flags under the clock . . . and those lights José has put up.

REMEDIOS   José is very handy.

DOROTEA   Yes, he is. He's a great help.

REMEDIOS   It's hard to believe. He looked so strange when he first arrived.

DOROTEA   He had his reasons. As did I... [*While she speaks, she moves about, rearranging the flowers and straightening the bottles on the counter.*]

BENITA   Of course... poor fellow...

REMEDIOS   [*Angry.*]   Everything seems all right to you since you found a suitor!

BENITA   Why shouldn't it? The poor man...

REMEDIOS   I heard that José was an actor. And that Juan was his agent.

DOROTEA   Perhaps. I never asked him. I'm not interested in what he has been, but what he is now. And José is a wonderful husband.

BENITA   And he's so handsome.

REMEDIOS   Will you be quiet, Benita? You're getting on my nerves.

BENITA   Of course, dear. I'm sorry.

REMEDIOS   Tell me something, Dorotea. Is it true that José has sold all seven of the houses you own?

DOROTEA   Seven, no. Six. He sold the old ones that couldn't be rented.

REMEDIOS   I heard that he's now in the process of disposing of the meat markets...

DOROTEA   Yes. They weren't doing very well. And since José knows a lot about these things...

REMEDIOS   I also heard that Juan sold his merry-go-round and is living off the proceeds. What does José do aside from putting up lights?

DOROTEA   He sleeps with me... loves me... we talk... we laugh. And we don't worry about what people think. Beyond that, he devotes himself to putting my affairs in order... they were something of a mess.

REMEDIOS   And he plays dominoes.

DOROTEA   Yes. He plays very well. As does Juan. They enjoy it on rainy days.

BENITA   Men always play well on rainy days.

REMEDIOS   I understand the stationmaster got quite angry at Juan the other day.

DOROTEA   [*Pretending interest.*]   Oh, really? I didn't know that. Tell me. This should be interesting.   [*She sits down to listen more attentively.*]

REMEDIOS   It seems that Juan said that people from Madrid played dominoes better than they do here.

DOROTEA   That's quite serious...

REMEDIOS   Of course it is. We have a reputation as domino players. Especially Don Felipe.

DOROTEA   How fascinating! And what else do you know?

BENITA   Yes, go on. . . tell us.

REMEDIOS   Well, I also know that you have forgiven your aunt and that you've given her one of your houses. And that you've put her in charge of the wine shop.

DOROTEA   That's true. When one is happy, one forgives. And I *am* happy, Remedios! Is there some other bit of information you want to give me?   [*She rises.*]

REMEDIOS   Well, since none of this seems to interest you!

DOROTEA   Not if it isn't about José.

REMEDIOS   Where is José, by the way?

DOROTEA   I don't know. . .he's out. . .but he'll be back soon. And I'll be here, waiting for him. Because I love him. Do you understand? And since you're in such a hurry and can't wait for his return, I'll give him your regards. Anything else?

REMEDIOS   No, nothing, Dorotea. . .

DOROTEA   Good-bye, then.   [*She kisses her on the cheek.*]

REMEDIOS   Good-bye, Dorotea.

BENITA   I'm glad you're happy.   [*Dorotea kisses her also.*]

REMEDIOS   I hope you're not making a mistake.

DOROTEA   I'm not making a mistake. Give my regards to Inés.

REMEDIOS   [*While moving toward the door, right.*]   Thank you, I will.

DOROTEA   Tell her I hope she gets over her pneumonia. . .

REMEDIOS   You see what love can do to you. As soon as she found a suitor, the poor thing stopped wearing her heavy coat. And look what happened.

DOROTEA   She'll get well. Good-bye, Reme. Beni.

BENITA   Good-bye.

REMEDIOS   Good-bye, Dorotea.   [*They exit right. Rosa enters left; she is very anxious.*]

ROSA   He hasn't come back yet, has he?   [*Dorotea reveals her own anxiety.*]

DOROTEA   No, Rosa. Today is the day he's leaving. I feel it. In my heart.

ROSA   But which one, Juan or José. That's what I'm not sure of.

DOROTEA   It has to be José. When I was brushing his coat, I found a ticket for Madrid in the pocket. He came in and surprised me, so I didn't have time to see the date, but it really doesn't matter. If it's not today, it will be tomorrow. He's leaving.

ROSA   The ticket could be his. . .or it could be Juan's.

DOROTEA   No, Rosa. It was in José's pocket; it was for him.

ROSA   How do you know Juan doesn't have one too? I haven't searched his pockets, but he's very nervous and upset. He keeps checking to see if the train to Madrid is on time. And he keeps pacing up and down the platform.

DOROTEA   But it was my husband who made two long distance tele-
phone calls yesterday. And I don't know to whom or why. And he's
very preoccupied. I've hardly seen him all day.

ROSA   Neither of them has packed a bag.

DOROTEA   They can leave without baggage, Rosa. Then they wouldn't
have to say good-bye. Simply get on the train and leave. That may
be why my friends came to see me. Perhaps they know
something. . .especially Remedios. . .

ROSA   But if it's José, you could stop him. . .

DOROTEA   No, I can't stop him. I understood from the beginning why he
came here. . .and accepted it. And I have too much pride to beg him
not to go. But it breaks my heart, Rosa. . .

ROSA   Quiet!   [*José enters right.*]

JOSÉ   Hello, you two.

DOROTEA   Hello, love. Where have you been?

JOSÉ   Just walking along the highway. Getting a little exercise. . .and
thinking.

DOROTEA   About what?

JOSÉ   About you.

DOROTEA   Truly?

JOSÉ   Of course.   [*To Rosa.*]   Where's Juan, Rosa?

ROSA   He's out on the platform.

JOSÉ   Do you know if the train is on time?

ROSA   It must be late.

DOROTEA   They haven't announced it yet.

JOSÉ   What have you two been up to?

DOROTEA   Oh, the usual. Some friends were by. . .

JOSÉ   What did they have to say?

DOROTEA   Nothing special. We just chatted. . .oh, they liked what we've
done to the restaurant. Especially the wall lights. . .

JOSÉ   [*Lost in thought.*]   Oh?

DOROTEA   What are you going to do, José?

JOSÉ   What do you mean?

DOROTEA   Until dinner. . .

JOSÉ   I don't know. I.think I'll go out to the platform.

DOROTEA   What for?

JOSÉ   You know how much I like to watch the trains. It was the only honest thing I told you that day, do you remember? I've always enjoyed
it. . .I like to see them go by.

DOROTEA   Do you want me to go with you?

JOSÉ   No, you'd probably get cold. Stay here. . .I'll be right back.

DOROTEA   Are you sure?

JOSÉ   Of course.

DOROTEA   José?

JOSÉ   Yes?

DOROTEA   Shall I make you a sandwich?

JOSÉ   A sandwich? Why?

DOROTEA   To take with you. In case you get hungry.

JOSÉ   Why should I get hungry?

DOROTEA   At least take a coat in case you get cold. Shall I have Rosa bring one down to you?

JOSÉ   [*Puzzled.*]   Are you all right?

DOROTEA   Yes.

JOSÉ   There's nothing the matter?

DOROTEA   No, nothing. I'm very happy. Aren't I, Rosa?

ROSA   Of course. This has been one of our better days.   [*The bell from the station rings.*]

DOROTEA   The bell.

ROSA   The train must be coming.

JOSÉ   I'd better go.

DOROTEA   Give me a kiss, José . . .

JOSÉ   Of course.   [*They kiss.*]   Good-bye.

DOROTEA   Good-bye.   [*José exits upstage. To Rosa, on the verge of tears.*]   You see?

ROSA   Yes.   [*Angry at the injustice of the situation.*]   They can't leave us this way. It's not right!   [*We hear the sound of the train.*]

DOROTEA   There's the train!

VOICE   [*Inside.*]   Zolitizola! Five minutes!

DOROTEA   Five minutes!

ROSA   Everything hinges on these minutes!

DOROTEA   No, Rosa. Because if it's not today, it will be tomorrow. He already has the ticket.   [*The bell rings again.*]

ROSA   Shall I look?

DOROTEA   Yes.   [*Rosa goes toward the upstage door, opens it slightly, then closes it.*]

ROSA   I'm afraid to.

DOROTEA   I know. If they've already decided, what good would it do?   [*We hear the whistle and the sound of the train leaving.*]

ROSA   The train is leaving.

DOROTEA   Yes.

ROSA   If only you hadn't let him sell everything!

DOROTEA   I owe my life to him, Rosa. Before he arrived, I was a hysterical woman on the verge of suicide. And he kept his promise of making me happy. Of being good to me. Even if he leaves today, I'm still indebted to him.   [*José enters from the rear door, visibly preoccupied.*]

JOSÉ   Hi.

ROSA   [*Turns, surprised.*]   Hello.

DOROTEA   [*Also surprised.*]   Hello.

JOSÉ   What's the matter?

ROSA   Oh, nothing.

DOROTEA   Nothing's the matter.

JOSÉ   Well, I'm back again. Has anyone been here?

DOROTEA   No, José. Were you expecting someone?

JOSÉ   I don't know...I thought someone might have gotten off the train.

ROSA   No, we haven't seen anyone.

JOSÉ   Not in the hotel either?   [*He goes toward the door on the left.*]

DOROTEA   No. No one.

ROSA   Not a soul.

JOSÉ   Was there a telegram for me?

DOROTEA   No.

JOSÉ   This is really odd...

ROSA   Why?

JOSÉ   Oh, nothing...but it is odd...

ROSA   [*Suddenly concerned, she goes toward José.*]   And Juan...where's Juan?

JOSÉ   Juan?

ROSA   Yes, where is he?

JOSÉ   The last time I saw him, he was with the stationmaster. They'd negotiated a truce and were getting ready to play another game of dominoes.

ROSA   Are you sure?

JOSÉ   Of course.

DOROTEA   Then he hasn't left?

JOSÉ   Where would he be going?

ROSA   I don't know...away...

JOSÉ   Well, he's with Don Felipe in his office. You can go see for yourself.

DOROTEA   Go on, Rosa. Go and see...

ROSA   [*To Dorotea.*]   Today is not the day.

DOROTEA   No, it's not today.

ROSA   I'm glad.

DOROTEA   So am I.

ROSA   At least it's one more day...   [*Exits upstage door.*]

JOSÉ   What's wrong with her?

DOROTEA   Nothing.

JOSÉ   She seemed nervous. And now that I think about it, so do you. Even when I was here before. What's wrong?

DOROTEA   What's wrong with you? You seem preoccupied. What's the matter?

JOSÉ   I have my reasons...

DOROTEA   What reasons?

JOSÉ   The truth is, I've been waiting for a friend, and he hasn't showed up. Juan and I were both waiting. He was supposed to be on the Madrid train, but he wasn't. I don't understand....I suppose he could have missed it and will be on the mail train at 10:30.

DOROTEA   And who is this friend you're expecting?

JOSÉ   Could I have a glass of wine? I'm really thirsty.

DOROTEA   Of course. I'll get it.   [*She goes behind the counter to serve the wine.*]

JOSÉ   I called Madrid yesterday and his wife told me he was in Bilbao and would be returning today. So I called him in Bilbao and asked him to stop here for the night. I hope you don't mind. You'll like him. He's married to a friend of mine, a singer I know. She's retired now but she was a very famous soprano...la Porcholes...you must have heard of her...Charito Porcholes...

DOROTEA   Why didn't you tell me you were waiting for this husband of...la Porcholes? Juan didn't say anything to Rosa, either.

JOSÉ   We wanted to surprise you.

DOROTEA   I don't understand.   [*José picks up the glass of wine and sits down at the table, left.*]

JOSÉ   Dorotea, we can't go on like this anymore....

DOROTEA   Like what, José?   [*She sits down beside him.*]

JOSÉ   This business of my being here with nothing to do. People are beginning to talk. And your friend Remedios has made some comments I really don't appreciate.

DOROTEA   [*Hopefully.*]   Do you care what the townspeople say?

JOSÉ   Of course I care! I play dominos with the priest and the pharmacist and with Don Felipe. These people are my friends. And I can't stay here without having something to do. It's embarrassing. And besides, I don't like it. And Juan doesn't either.

DOROTEA   So what are you planning to do?

JOSÉ   Could I have another glass of wine, please?

DOROTEA   Of course, José. But go on...   [*Dorotea goes toward the counter to get the wine.*]

JOSÉ   You know we have some capital from the houses I've sold. And we'll have even more when we get rid of the businesses that aren't doing well...

DOROTEA   Yes.

JOSÉ   Well, Juan and I have a great idea...

DOROTEA   Tell me.

JOSÉ   That was going to be our surprise. But I wanted to talk to my friend first.

DOROTEA   Can't you tell me anything about it?   [*She returns with the glass of wine, which she offers to José.*]

JOSÉ   Well, just outside of town there's some land we can buy at a good price. I took a look at it again just this afternoon. It's got trees and a view of the sea. And what we thought was that we could build a first-class restaurant there. An inn or something of that sort, you know, with very high prices. Tourists are beginning to discover this town. It wouldn't surprise me, providing the weather continues to be outrageously disagreeable, if it didn't end up being the latest place to go.

DOROTEA   That's possible.

JOSÉ   Next to the restaurant, we'd put some swings and a merry-go-round and some rides, the kind of thing Juan knows how to run. And I'd be in charge of all the rest. . .and you would too, of course. . .

DOROTEA   [*With increasing emotion.*]   Yes, José.

JOSÉ   La Porcholes's husband is a contractor, and I thought he could do all the building. That's why I asked him to come here—to see the lot and draw up some plans. . .

DOROTEA   Do you think he's going to come?

JOSÉ   Well, he told me to get him a ticket to Madrid   [*taking a ticket from his pocket*]   for tomorrow. If he weren't coming, he'd have sent me a telegram. . .

DOROTEA   Of course.   [*She gets up so that José cannot see that she's crying.*]

JOSÉ   Where are you going?

DOROTEA   To get you some French fries.   [*She goes behind the counter.*]

JOSÉ   Thank you. I thought on Sundays, we could have an orchestra at dinner. . .and we could ask my friend to sing. She's told me how much she misses performing. She's a little heavy now, of course, but she'd really enjoy it. And each Sunday or holiday we could invite a different artist.

DOROTEA   And you. . .wouldn't you like to sing sometime?   [*She returns to the table with the plate.*]

JOSÉ   Well, it's possible that someday, if the public demands it, I might do something. It's not that I want to go back to my old profession, but it might bring in a few people and be good for business. After all, the name José Rivadavia hasn't been totally forgotten.

DOROTEA   It'll never be forgotten.

JOSÉ   And I've even thought of a name for the place. We could call it The Enchanting Dorotea. What do you think?

DOROTEA   It's marvelous.   [*She rises again to hide her feelings.*]

JOSÉ   Where are you going?

DOROTEA   To get more French fries.   [*She goes behind the counter again.*]

JOSÉ   What's wrong? Are you crying?   [*He stands facing her, across the counter.*]

DOROTEA   José...can you forgive me? For days I've been tormented by the idea that you were leaving. Do you understand? And it wasn't just that you were leaving, but that my pride, my arrogance, my enormous cowardice kept me from following you wherever you went and begging you to stay with me.

JOSÉ   I never thought of leaving, Dorotea.

DOROTEA   That's why you have to forgive me – for distrusting you, for forgetting that life may not be as dark as it sometimes seems, and that though there are ugly days, there are also times, like today, of great joy.   [*At that moment, we hear a loud thunderclap followed by a gust of wind.*]

JOSÉ   Did you hear that?

DOROTEA   Yes.   [*Lyrically.*]   It's the galerna! The west wind.

JOSÉ   [*Ignoring the bad weather.*]   The Enchanting Dorotea. Do you like it?

DOROTEA   It will be the most beautiful inn ever! And it would be worth it if only to let you and la Porcholes hear the applause you deserve. Would you like a cognac, José?

JOSÉ   Yes, a cognac, please, Dorotea.   [*Dorotea serves the cognac while the storm continues, then the storm is mixed with the sound of a passing train.*]

THE END